The Epistle of Paul the Apostle
to the Colossians

The Epistle of Paul the Apostle to the Colossians

by
Oliver B. Greene

The Gospel Hour, Inc., Oliver B. Greene, Director
P. O. Box 2024, Greenville, South Carolina

First printing, September 1963

Second printing, March 1964

Library of Congress Catalog Card Number: 63-21467

This volume is dedicated to all
"To whom God would make known what is the riches of the glory of this mystery among the Gentiles; which is Christ in you, the hope of glory: Whom we preach, warning every man, and teaching every man in all wisdom; that we may present every man perfect in Christ Jesus: Whereunto I also labour, striving according to his working, which worketh in me mightily."

Colossians 1:27—29

THE EPISTLE OF PAUL THE APOSTLE
TO THE COLOSSIANS

INTRODUCTION

Historians tell us that Colosse was a celebrated city of Phrygia, in Asia Minor, "a city well inhabited, and large." The historian Pliny tells us that Colosse, Laodicea, and Hierapolis were at the same time overwhelmed and destroyed by a great earthquake in the latter part of the reign of Nero, not long after this Epistle was written. Colosse recovered and was rebuilt. The ancient town is now extinct, but its site is occupied by a village called Chonas—or, as some spell it—Khonas. The village is picturesque and beautifully situated in the valley near Mount Cadmus.

The village now situated where Colosse once stood is approached through beautiful country, rugged and wild. In the immediate neighborhood are several small communities, and among them can be found the ruins of arches, vaults, and giant squared stones. The ground is literally strewn with broken pottery which is often found near and around the ruins of these old Bible cities. Arches, vaults and pieces of broken pottery are all that now remains of the city of Colosse where the church was established, and to which Paul directed the Colossian Epistle.

In Acts 15:40—41 and Acts 16:1—6, we learn that the Gospel was first preached in Phrygia by Paul, Silas and Timothy. The Scriptures tell us that they went throughout Phrygia, which would indicate that they went into all the principal cities and towns in that area. In Acts 18:23 we learn that Paul visited this area again after he had preached in Philippi, Athens and Jerusalem; and at the same time, he visited Antioch. At that time,

Paul "went over all the country of Galatia and Phrygia in order, strengthening all the disciples."

The Word of God does not specifically state that Paul and Silas went to the city of Colosse, but since that city was one of the outstanding cities in Phrygia, there is no reason to doubt that they did visit Colosse and preach the Gospel there.

Some teachers have suggested that Paul probably did not establish the church at Colosse, but in Colossians 1:21–25 he says, in effect, that he himself preached the Gospel to the Colossians. The salutations at the end of the Epistle, directed to various persons in Laodicea and Colosse, show that Paul was personally acquainted with these individuals, and there is no doubt in my mind that he founded the church in Colosse and was the first to preach the Gospel of the marvelous grace of God to the people there.

In chapter 4, verses 7 and 8, it is said that the Epistle to the Colossians was sent by Tychicus and Onesimus, both of whom are commended as being "faithful and beloved brethren." The Epistle contains remarks which prove without a doubt that Paul wrote it while in prison at Rome. In chapter 1:24 Paul says, "Who now rejoice in my sufferings for you." Again, in chapter 4:18, we read, *"Remember my bonds."* From these statements it is not difficult to fix the date of the writing of the Epistle to the Colossians, certainly with some degree of accuracy. It was written about 62 A. D., at approximately the same time as the Epistles to the Ephesians and Philemon, and is believed to have been delivered by the same messengers.

OCCASION OF THE EPISTLE – WHY WRITTEN

The Epistle to the Colossians strongly resembles the Epistle to the Ephesians, and was written in view of the errors which were numerous and prevalent in the churches in that part of Asia Minor. The church at Colosse was one of a circle of churches near each other in that particular area, and it is probable that the same general religious views and doctrines and the same errors prevailed throughout the entire region where they were situated.

The group of churches there included Ephesus, Laodicea, Thyatira and Colosse and in general those addressed in Revelation as "the seven churches of Asia." There were several groups at that time who taught various errors within the limits of the churches of Asia Minor. In Ephesus there were those "who say they are apostles, and are not" (Rev. 2:2b). In the church at Smyrna were those "who say they are Jews, and are not, but are the synagogue of Satan" (Rev. 2:9). In the church at Thyatira "that woman Jezebel, which calleth herself a prophetess" was allowed to teach (Rev. 2:20). In Pergamos were those who held the doctrine of the Nicolaitanes (Rev. 2:15), and also those who held the doctrine of Balaam (Rev. 2:14). These churches were quite near Colosse, and probably the people were partakers of these errors—at least in part.

When Paul departed from Ephesus, he gave warning against a dangerous group of teachers who would come into the area: "For I know this, that after my departing shall grievous wolves enter in among you, not sparing the flock. Also of your own selves shall men arise, speaking perverse things, to draw away disciples after them" (Acts 20:29,30). Paul does not spell out the kind of danger to which the believers at Ephesus would be exposed, but no doubt he referred to the practice of mixing Law and grace, thus teaching a religion of works, days, and tradition of men—instead of the grace of God, the shed blood, and the resurrected, living Saviour.

In that part of Asia Minor there had been quite a number of John the Baptist's disciples, who retained many Jewish prejudices and observances of the Mosaic Law. What their views were, what part of the Law they clung to, is not specifically named; but it is clear that these disciples of John regarded the Jewish Law as binding, and that they held to rigid observance of some of the rituals and feast days as taught by Mosaic Law. They refused to accept salvation by grace through faith— minus Law, minus works, minus anything man can do.

When Paul came to Ephesus he found quite a number of these disciples of John. They professed that they did not know there was a Holy Ghost, and that they were baptized only unto John's baptism (Acts 19:1–3). Paul preached the Gospel of Grace to these people, told them about the Spirit, and they received the Holy Ghost as did others whom Paul enlightened concerning the dispensation of the grace of God.

There was a distinguished and very influential disciple of John in that region (Acts 18:24,25). His name was Apollos, and we are told that he was a mighty man in the Scriptures and that he taught the things of the Lord at Ephesus. Although he was an honest and sincere man, we do not know how long he taught before he was made more fully acquainted with the Gospel of pure grace. What Apollos taught is not specifically outlined, but his teaching contributed noticeably to the confusion and misunderstanding existing in that area when Paul came preaching pure grace minus works, Law or traditions of men. Acts 18:26 tells us that "the way of God was expounded more perfectly" to Apollos, but what he taught *before* the way of God was expounded more perfectly to him, we do not know. We might believe that he was mixing Law and works with grace, for we must bear in mind that this was the transition period, and some of the Jews were reluctant to break away completely from Judaism and the Law of Moses. God called Paul as a special apostle with a special message to correct the error of grace plus Law. As we study Colossians we will see one by one the errors which Paul set about to correct by preaching Jesus Christ and the grace of God. He warned concerning the danger and the influence of philosophy (Col. 2:4–8). He warned the believers to beware lest anyone should "beguile you with enticing words." He cautioned them concerning "philosophy and vain deceit." (Paul was referring here to a philosophy based on tradition of men, after the rudiments of the world, and not after Christ.) Such a philosophy might be expected to prevail in Colosse, located so near Greece, since Athens was the center of both culture and idolatry.

Paul also referred to those who insisted on observing rites, customs, days, feasts, etc., as having to do with Judaism and the Jewish religion. In chapter 2:16 he says: "Let no man therefore judge you in meat, or in drink, or in respect of an holy day, or of the new moon, or of the sabbath days." No doubt there were religious leaders in Colosse attempting to force the believers to observe the Jewish rituals and holy days. Paul set about to correct this error.

There is also some evidence of the prevalence of a philosophy more oriental than that of Greece—a philosophy leaning toward Gnosticism. This philosophy was the foundation of a large part of the error in the church at Colosse. Paul's message was to assure the people that in Christ all the fullness of the Godhead dwelt bodily. Since Paul emphasized this fact so forcefully, it would seem that there probably were some who denied the fullness of the Godhead, denying that Jesus was God in flesh. Such denial was a favorite doctrine of the Gnostics in that particular day. Gnosticism taught that the human nature of the Son of God was not in reality, but *in appearance only*. They taught that He did not *die* in reality, but in appearance only. Therefore, in chapter 2:18 we read of "a voluntary humility and worshipping of angels, intruding into those things which he hath not seen," and which tend to vainly puff up a fleshly mind.

In this verse we have a description which certainly applies with remarkable accuracy to the homage paid by the Gnostics to the aeons, and to the general efforts of those who held the doctrine of that philosophy. To intrude into those things which are not seen (we might say the secret things which belong unto God) and to offer an explanation of the mode of divine existence and the nature of divine agency, gave these people a philosophy that denied God in the flesh in the person of the Lord Jesus Christ.

WE believe Jesus WAS *God in flesh* (II Cor. 5:19), and that in Him dwelt the fullness of the Godhead bodily. We believe the secret things belong unto the Lord our God, and the things which are revealed belong to us. We are not to speculate, we are not to intrude where angels fear to tread: "The secret things belong unto the Lord our God: but those things which are revealed belong unto us and to our children for ever, that we may do all the words of this law" (Deut. 29:29).

You will notice that Paul does not rebuke the believers at Colosse in regard to their morals and the religious character of the members of the assembly there. There is no mention of improper conduct, either on the part of individuals or on the part of the church at large. (Such is not true concerning the church at Corinth. Paul rebuked the Corinthians sternly concerning their morals and conduct in the church.) There is no suggestion in the Epistle to the Colossians that they were guilty of sins common to all heathen in that day. It is suggested however, that they were *exposed* to gross sin, and there are solemn charges against *indulging* in sin, the lust of the flesh, and the pride of life. The sins to which they were exposed were such as prevailed in all the ancient cities; but the people in the Colossian church were not guilty, and Paul did not rebuke them concerning sins practiced by unbelievers in that day.

Sins prevalent in that area at that time were "fornication, uncleanness, inordinate affection, evil concupiscence, and covetousness, which is idolatry . . . anger, wrath, malice, blasphemy, filthy communication . . . and lying" (Col. 3:5–9). If you will study the first chapter of Romans you will discover that these sins were common among the heathen in Paul's day. (They are still common among the heathen—and sad but so, they are also common among civilized people in our day!)

Colossians 3:7 suggests that these believers at Colosse had presented their bodies a living sacrifice, and had surrendered their members as instruments of righteousness. Paul says, "In the which ye also walked SOME TIME, WHEN YE LIVED IN THEM. BUT NOW YE ALSO PUT OFF ALL THESE."

The paramount reason for the Epistle to the Colossians was to guard the believers in the church against the errors to which they were exposed—errors that were so pronounced and prominent in that particular country—false philosophy, the influence of false teachers in religion, those who asserted their *superiority* in religion, and those who taught Jewish customs of holy days, holidays and feast days as practiced by Judaizers.

As we study Colossians we will note a remarkable similarity to the book of Ephesians. The two Epistles have much in common—in fact, the resemblance between the two is greater than exists between any of the other Pauline epistles. This resemblance is noticeable not only in general style and manner, but also in course of thought. The arguments set forth, the particular instructions given, and some of the phrases that are used in these two Epistles are not found anywhere else in Paul's writings. Let me point out just a few similarities between the Epistle to the Ephesians and the Epistle to the Colossians:

First—there is similarity as having to do with the reason for Paul's imprisonment at Rome. He was not in Rome simply for preaching Christianity in general—but because he preached that the Gentiles had the right to be admitted to the church on equal footing with Jews and without conforming to Jewish Law, rituals, etc. The doctrine of pure grace for Jew and Gentile alike was the doctrine to which he considered himself a martyr. In Colossians 1:24 he says, "Who now rejoice in my sufferings for you." Again in Colossians 2:1 he says, "For I would that ye knew what great conflict I have for you, and for them at Laodicea." Paul's conflicts and trials in prison, his danger of being murdered at any moment, had occurred because of his attempt to spread the Gospel and preach Jesus Christ—crucified, buried, and risen— the only hope of salvation . . . ("Christ in you, the hope of glory.")

The preaching of this doctrine at Colosse and Laodicea had caused him to be thrown into jail, tried, convicted—and now he was waiting patiently for that day when his head would drop into the headsman's basket and he would seal his testimony with his life's blood. His message most hated was the message of pure grace— minus Law, minus works; just faith in the shed blood and the finished work of the Lord Jesus Christ.

God called Paul to be a minister to the Gentiles:

"For I speak to you Gentiles, inasmuch as I am the apostle of the Gentiles, I magnify mine office" (Rom. 11:13). These communities where Paul was preaching were Gentile communities, and he had been thrown in prison because of his efforts to preach to the Gentiles and convert them to the Lord God Almighty, preaching that they had the same right as the Jew and that they could be saved *apart from Judaism or any part of the Law.*

In Ephesians 3:1 he said, "For this cause I Paul, the prisoner of Jesus Christ for you Gentiles . . . ." Here he clearly states that he is in jail for preaching to the Gentiles, and the Ephesus letter was written at the same time as the letter to the believers at Colosse.

In Colossians 4:3 we read, "Withal praying also for us, that God would open unto us a door of utterance, to speak the mystery of Christ, for which I am also in bonds." The mystery of Christ for which Paul was in bonds is clearly defined in his letter to the church at Ephesus: "Whereby, when ye read, ye may understand my knowledge in the mystery of Christ which in other ages was not made known unto the sons of men, as it is now revealed unto His holy apostles and prophets by the Spirit; that the Gentiles should be fellowheirs, and of the same body, and partakers of His promise in Christ by the Gospel" (Eph. 3:4–6).

In Acts 21:27–31 the same statement is made in regard to the reason for Paul's persecution and imprisonment: "And when the seven days were almost ended, the Jews which were of Asia, when they saw him in the temple, stirred up all the people, and laid hands on him, crying out, Men of Israel, help: This is the man, that teacheth all men every where against the people, and the law, and this place: and further brought Greeks also into the temple, and hath polluted this holy place. (For they had seen before with him in the city Trophimus an

Ephesian, whom they supposed that Paul had brought into the temple.) And all the city was moved, and the people ran together: and they took Paul, and drew him out of the temple: and forthwith the doors were shut. And as they went about to kill him, tidings came unto the chief captain of the band, that all Jerusalem was in an uproar."

Acts 22:21—24 gives the following account of Paul's defence before the multitude: "And He said unto me, Depart: for I will send thee far hence unto the Gentiles. And they gave him audience unto this word, and then lifted up their voices, and said, Away with such a fellow from the earth: for it is not fit that he should live. And as they cried out, and cast off their clothes, and threw dust into the air, the chief captain commanded him to be brought into the castle, and bade that he should be examined by scourging; that he might know wherefore they cried so against him."

These passages teach us that one thing which caused Paul's people to hate him and which drew down the vengeance of his countrymen upon him was the fact that he preached to the Gentiles, declaring unto them that they could be saved by grace through faith, and be admitted to the privileges of salvation and heaven by faith in the finished work of Jesus *minus the deeds of the Law*. The Jews said he was not fit to live. They went into a tantrum, threw dust into the air and would have killed Paul had they gotten their hands on Him. But God protected him because He had more work for him to do.

A VERY INTERESTING COMPARISON

The comparison between Colossians and Ephesians is very interesting and profitable, as the following Scriptures will prove:

Ephesians 1:15—19   and   Colossians 1:9—11

Ephesians 1:20–23 and Colossians 1:15–19
Ephesians 1:10 and Colossians 1:20
Ephesians 2:1–10 and Colossians 1:21–23
Ephesians 3:7 and Colossians 1:25
Ephesians 3:9,10 and Colossians 1:26,27
Ephesians 3:17 and Colossians 2:7
Ephesians 2:11–22 and Colossians 2:11–15
Ephesians 4:14 and Colossians 2:8
Ephesians 4:15,16 and Colossians 2:19
Ephesians 4:25 and Colossians 3:9
Ephesians 4:22–24 and Colossians 3:9,10
Ephesians 4:32 and Colossians 3:12,13
Ephesians 5:19,20 and Colossians 3:16,17
Ephesians 5:21–25; 6:1–9 and Colossians 3:18–24; 4:1
Ephesians 6:19 and Colossians 4:3
Ephesians 5:16 and Colossians 4:5
Ephesians 6:21,22 and Colossians 4:7,8

Comparison of these passages reveals a striking resemblance between the two. We are therefore led to believe that similar conditions existed in the two churches. They were exposed to similar dangers concerning religious error.

There is another very remarkable thing about Ephesians and Colossians: It is only in these two epistles that Paul solemnly warns believers about *lying*:

"Wherefore, putting away lying, speak every man truth with his neighbour; for we are members one of another" (Eph. 4:25).

"Lie not one to another, seeing that ye have put off the old man with his deeds" (Col. 3:9).

We conclude that lying was one of the sins that prevailed in the region where these churches were situated. Probably the members of the churches at Ephesus and Colosse had been addicted to the vice of lying before their conversion, and Paul sternly warns against it. I feel there is a deeper meaning here: The most subtle liar of all is a *religious liar!* The dirtiest thief this side of hell is a religious thief—one who would lie and thus damn your soul. The devil is the father of lies . . . he lied to Eve, she succumbed, and he is still in the lying business. Through his subtle lies he has populated hell and is still sending millions there. Jesus is truth (John 17:17; 14:6). "Ye shall know the truth, and the truth shall make you free" (John 8:32; 8:36).

The devil is a lie—exactly the opposite of Jesus: ". . . God shall send them strong delusion, that they should believe (the) Lie: That they all might be damned who believed not the truth, but had pleasure in unrighteousness" (II Thess. 2:11,12). The literal Greek here should be translated not "*A* lie," but "THE Lie"—*the devil*; and if you listen to *The Lie* you will be damned!

We can sum up the theme of Colossians in the following words: So far as the fundamentals of the faith are concerned, the church at Colosse was in excellent condition (Col. 1:3–8). There were two forms of very subtle error at work: The first was legality in the Alexandrian form of asceticism . . . "touch not, taste not." There was also a trace of Judaism—the observance of days, feasts, new moons, etc. The second form of subtle error was false mysticism ("intruding into those things which he hath not seen"), which was the result of philosophic speculation.

Because of these ever present dangers, Paul wrote the Epistle to the Colossians. However, it was not written for that day only, but also for a warning to believers today. "All Scripture is given by inspiration of God, and is profitable for doctrine, for reproof, for correction, for instruction in righteousness: That the man of God may be perfect, throughly furnished unto all good works" (II Tim. 3:16,17).

CONTENTS

COLOSSIANS -- CHAPTER ONE

1. Paul, an apostle of Jesus Christ by the will of God, and Timotheus our brother,

2. To the saints and faithful brethren in Christ which are at Colosse: Grace be unto you, and peace, from God our Father and the Lord Jesus Christ.

3. We give thanks to God and the Father of our Lord Jesus Christ, praying always for you,

4. Since we heard of your faith in Christ Jesus, and of the love which ye have to all the saints,

5. For the hope which is laid up for you in heaven, whereof ye heard before in the word of the truth of the gospel;

6. Which is come unto you, as it is in all the world; and bringeth forth fruit, as it doth also in you, since the day ye heard of it, and knew the grace of God in truth:

7. As ye also learned of Epaphras our dear fellowservant, who is for you a faithful minister of Christ;

8. Who also declared unto us your love in the Spirit.

9. For this cause we also, since the day we heard it, do not cease to pray for you, and to desire that ye might be filled with the knowledge of his will in all wisdom and spiritual understanding;

10. That ye might walk worthy of the Lord unto all pleasing, being fruitful in every good work, and increasing in the knowledge of God;

11. Strengthened with all might, according to his glorious power, unto all patience and longsuffering with joyfulness;

12. Giving thanks unto the Father, which hath made us meet to be partakers of the inheritance of the saints in light:

13. Who hath delivered us from the power of darkness, and hath translated us into the kingdom of his dear Son:

14. In whom we have redemption through his blood, even the forgiveness of sins:

15. Who is the image of the invisible God, the firstborn of every creature:

16. For by him were all things created, that are in heaven, and that are in earth, visible and invisible, whether they be thrones, or dominions, or principalities, or powers: all things were created by him, and for him:

17. And he is before all things, and by him all things consist.

18. And he is the head of the body, the church: who is the beginning, the firstborn from the dead; that in all things he

might have the preeminence.

19. For it pleased the Father that in him should all fulness dwell;

20. And, having made peace through the blood of his cross, by him to reconcile all things unto himself; by him, I say, whether they be things in earth, or things in heaven.

21. And you, that were sometime alienated and enemies in your mind by wicked works, yet now hath he reconciled

22. In the body of his flesh through death, to present you holy and unblameable and unreproveable in his sight:

23. If ye continue in the faith grounded and settled, and be not moved away from the hope of the gospel, which ye have heard, and which was preached to every creature which is under heaven; whereof I Paul am made a minister;

24. Who now rejoice in my sufferings for you, and fill up that which is behind of the afflictions of Christ in my flesh for his body's sake, which is the church:

25. Whereof I am made a minister, according to the dispensation of God which is given to me for you, to fulfil the word of God;

26. Even the mystery which hath been hid from ages and from generations, but now is made manifest to his saints:

27. To whom God would make known what is the riches of the glory of this mystery among the Gentiles; which is Christ in you, the hope of glory:

28. Whom we preach, warning every man, and teaching every man in all wisdom; that we may present every man perfect in Christ Jesus:

29. Whereunto I also labour, striving according to his working, which worketh in me mightily.

As we study chapter one, we will find the following:

1. Salutation to the church at Colosse — verses 1 and 2.

2. Thanks to God for what He had done in giving His only begotten Son for the Colossians (the Gentiles as well as the Jews), and thanks for fruits produced by hearing the Gospel — verses 3—8.

3. Paul's prayer on behalf of the Colossians, that they might persevere in the same course and walk worthy of the high calling of God in Christ Jesus — verses 9—11.

4.   Paul's exhortation to the Colossians to render thanks
     to God for what He had done for them in sending
Christ to redeem them from the curse of sin and the Law
— verses 12–14.

5.   A statement describing the exalted dignity of our Re-
     deemer, the Lord Jesus Christ — verses 15–18.

6.   A statement of the work done by the Lord Jesus in
     redeeming us and making peace by the blood of His
cross, and *by the blood* reconciling the world to God —
verses 19 and 20.

7.   Through the Gospel Paul preached—grace, pure grace—
     we are told that sinners have been reconciled to God,
and through reconciliation (redemption that is in His blood)
we are now brought into a state wherein we can be presented to the Father, holy and unblameable, without spot
— verses 21–23.

8.   Paul declares himself a minister of this Gospel of
     grace . . . the Gospel of reconciliation and redemp-
tion . . . the Gospel that makes us fit for the Kingdom.
Because of the preaching of this Gospel, Paul declares
that he had been called upon to endure trials, sufferings,
imprisonment; but those trials were a joy—and in preaching the Gospel he had been, was, and would be diligent,
warning every man . . . teaching every man in all wisdom,
that he might present everyone perfect *in Christ Jesus* —
verses 24–29.

INTRODUCTION AND GREETING

Verse 1:   "Paul, *an apostle of Jesus Christ by the
will of God*, and Timotheus our brother." Here, as always, Paul wants us to clearly understand that he is not
an apostle by his own choosing, nor by man's election—
but that he was called, ordained, commissioned, and sent
by God . . . "the apostle of Jesus Christ." Paul clearly

distinguishes between himself and Timothy, who is a brother and fellow labourer, but not an apostle.

There is a very definite reason why Paul associates Timothy with the Epistle to the Colossians. Timothy was a native of the area where the Colossian church was located (Acts 16:1–3). He had been with Paul when the Apostle preached the Gospel there, and no doubt was well known to the Colossian people (Acts 16:6). It is true, however, from the manner in which Paul mentions him, that he did not regard him as a fellow apostle, but rather as a co-worker and his son in the ministry.

In Philippians 1:1 we read, "Paul and Timotheus, *the servants* of Jesus Christ." Read I Thessalonians 1:1 and II Thessalonians 1:1. Had Paul regarded Timothy as having apostolic authority, he would not have differentiated between Timothy and himself as he did in the letters to the churches.

Paul had godly jealousy for the churches he founded. I am not referring to jealousy in a sinful manner; but God is a jealous God, and Paul was jealous for his people. He wanted to be regarded as their leader and the final authority on what should be preached in the church at Colosse.

Paul was an apostle of Jesus Christ. He bore His commission, enjoyed His inspiration, did His work, and IN ALL THINGS SOUGHT HIS ACCEPTANCE. Timothy is also found in the Second Epistle to the Corinthinas, and in Philippians and Philemon. He and Silvanus are mentioned in the salutations of both letters addressed to the believers in Thessalonica. In I Thessalonians 3:2 Paul refers to Timothy as a minister of God and a fellow laborer in the Gospel of Christ. Timothy received his Greek name from his father; his mother was a Jewess. In all probability they were natives of

21

Lystra (Acts 16:1). Timothy was undoubtedly Paul's convert, because Paul referred to him lovingly as "son," "my own son," "my beloved son," "my dearly beloved son" (I Tim. 1:18; 1:2; I Cor. 4:17; II Tim. 1:2). Young Timothy was well reported by all the brethren. He enjoyed an early religious education which was fundamental and sound. He learned the truth from his mother and his grandmother, as well as at the feet of the Apostle Paul. Paul selected him to be his fellow traveler and co-laborer, and gave this testimony concerning him: *"He worketh the work of the Lord*, as I also do" (I Cor. 16:10).

On another occasion, Paul declared that both Timothy and himself preached the same identical Gospel of the Son of God—pure grace (II Cor. 1:19). Certainly a kindred spirit reigned within these two, so closely knit together in love for the Gospel. To the church in Philippi Paul said, "I trust in the Lord Jesus to send Timotheus shortly unto you, that I also may be of good comfort, when I know your state. *For I have no man likeminded, who will naturally care for your state*" (Phil. 2:19,20). Timothy was Paul's brother in Christ, helping the Apostle in his work, carrying his messages for him, bringing correspondence to him. He was endeared to Paul in so many ways, and represented him in his absence from the church at Colosse. No wonder that in the very first verse of the Epistle Paul mentions *"Timotheus, our brother!"*

Verse 2: "To the saints and faithful brethren in Christ which are at Colosse: Grace be unto you, and peace, from God our Father and the Lord Jesus Christ."

The literal translation reads, "To those in Colosse who are saints and believing brethren in Christ." All born again, blood-washed believers are saints. Recently a certain religion promoted a person to sainthood who has been dead for many years. Such practice has no basis in Scripture. *God has only saints!* Every born again, blood-washed child of God is a saint! When we become partakers of salvation in Christ Jesus, we are that split second transformed from sinner to saint. There is no gradual attaining of sainthood. Good works do not make saints of us, and no man (or group of men) has any right to promote a person to sainthood after that person is dead!

All believers are saints "and faithful brethren in Christ." When we are covered by the blood we are just as pure, holy and spotless as the blood that covers us! God has nothing BUT saints in His family. All Christians are children of one Father, and by faith in Christ the entire family of God is rightly called "saints" and "believing brethren."

". . . Grace be unto you, and peace, from God our Father and the Lord Jesus Christ."

In verses 3 through 7, Paul expresses his deep gratitude to God the Father for the Colossian church. He thanks God for the faith, love, hope—and for the fruits of that Gospel which Epaphras had so successfully preached to them and had so thoroughly taught them. He then repeats the substance of the prayer he had offered for these believers—a sevenfold prayer that closes in a declaration of the believer's obligation to and connection with Christ. To Paul, the blessed name of Jesus suggested a magnificent description of the *majesty* of Jesus— His person, the glory of His work as the Great Creator; the Preserver and *only Redeemer* of mankind; the ruler and governor over all—yea, all in heaven and in earth!

Verse 3: "We give thanks to God and the Father of our Lord Jesus Christ, praying always for you."

"We" in verse three probably refers to Paul and Timothy. Paul is directing thanks where it should be directed: "We thank *God*, the Father of our Lord Jesus Christ." It is God, the Father of Christ, whom we should thank, for in His relationship to us He is *our God*—but He is also *our Father*. He is the Father of our Christ, our Saviour; we are heirs of God and joint heirs with *Christ*; therefore, in the sight of God, we have the same standing as Christ the Son, and God is our Father-God. The Spirit-directed heart pours itself out to God in praises and thanksgiving. I believe in shouting Christianity—but some of the shouting and public demonstrations we hear and see today are many times put on to display one's zeal or holiness. True shouting is done in secret.

Paul was pouring out praises and thanksgiving to God even though he was chained in a Roman prison cell. Why was he so happy? It was because he and Timothy had heard of the spiritual growth of the church at Colosse, and instead of congratulating each other on their fine work among the Colossians, *they both glorified God.* Their hearts poured out praises and thanksgiving to God for the spiritual progress the Colossians were making. The hearts of Paul and Timothy were so closely knit together in love and fellowship that Paul did not hesitate to say, "WE give thanks to God."

". . . Praying always for you." Paul prayed continually for the believers at Colosse, so deep was his interest in them, so great was his sympathy with and for them. He bore them always on his heart, and from his heart he carried them to the throne of grace in ceaseless prayer. "The effectual fervent prayer of a righteous man availeth much," even though he be in jail, cut off bodily from their presence. In his far-off prison, praying for the Colossians, Paul was like the prophet Elijah on Mount Carmel. Elijah prayed—and a little cloud appeared . . . a very small cloud; but as it gradually filled and darkened the horizon there was the sound of abundance of rain! Paul prayed the effectual fervent prayer of a righteous man, and such a prayer always brings abundance—regardless of whether the need be rain, grace, strength, mercy . . . or "whatsoever God supplieth."

Verse 4: "Since we heard of your faith in Christ Jesus, and of the love which ye have to all the saints . . . ." Paul was in prison, but he had received the good news through Epaphras, who was his co-laborer in the Colossian church. His heart was gladdened exceedingly by the news of their consistency, spiritual growth and advancement. With a heart full of joy, he offered thanks to God for the Colossian Christians.

Paul was grateful to God that the Colossians were demonstrating their love *toward all saints.* Heaven knows that in this cold world today we need a revival that will plant love in the hearts of saints one for another. This is the age of factions, and the saints of God are so busy splitting theological hairs over some doctrine or dogma that they do not have time to be affectionate one toward another, nor to demonstrate the love the Colossians were demonstrating to all saints. Please note: Not to *all men* as such, but to *all saints.*

Verse 5: "For the hope which is laid up for you in heaven, whereof ye heard before in the word of the truth of the gospel." Notice in verses 4 and 5, Paul speaks of faith, love, and hope: "Your faith . . . love which ye have to all the saints . . . for the hope which is laid up for you in heaven."

The literal Greek here reads, "Having heard of your faith in Christ Jesus, and the love which you have to all the saints, as often as we pray for you, we thank God, the Father of our Lord Jesus Christ, on account of the hope laid up for you in heaven." In essence, that is to say, the report Paul had received of their faith and love prompted the Apostle to give thanks to God and pour out praises to Him; but as Paul poured out thanksgiving and praises to God, the final issue and crown of those graces rose into prominence before him and he hastened to add, "ON ACCOUNT OF THE HOPE LAID UP FOR YOU IN HEAVEN." Their faith and their love are not viewed by Paul only in the present, at that moment, but he saw beyond that moment to the ultimate bliss they would inherit because they had believed on the Lord Jesus Christ and were bearing spiritual fruits that proved their experience genuine. Their ultimate blessing was the real ground of thanksgiving in the heart of the Apostle as he sat in the Roman jail.

Paul says practically the same thing in Ephesians 1:18: "The eyes of your understanding being enlightened; that ye may know what is the hope of His calling, and what the riches of the glory of His inheritance in the saints." Here the object hoped for is seen. We have in this verse the idea of security and reservation in heaven—and not that we have joy, love and peace now *only*. Read Luke 19:20; II Timothy 4:8; I Peter 1:4.

It is true that we DO have *joy* now, but the *hope* that we have is kept in store; we will possess it in that day when we receive our inheritance which is now reserved and kept in heaven. It is laid up *"in the heavens . . ."* in regions of splendor at God's right hand where God Himself guards it. Our inheritance is in the presence of Christ, who purchased it for us and who will bestow it upon us. Our heavenly glory is the object of hope to those of us who possess faith and who have trusted the Lord Jesus with all of our heart, depending upon His shed blood and finished work for the remission of sin, for our keeping and for our eternal reward.

We are redeemed NOW—but we live looking forward to *"the hope of His calling . . . the riches of the glory of His inheritance in the saints"* (Eph. 1:18). This glorious hope is future; it is not yet enjoyed by us, but is reserved and waiting for us. Hope that is seen is not hope. This future hope that true believers have is the unimagined, unknowable glory of spiritual perfection such as Jesus alone could provide for us . . . the hope of living in the unshaded radiance of God's glorious face; the hope of that day when we will enjoy uninterrupted fellowship with God, the Father of our Lord and Saviour Jesus Christ.

This holds for us the anticipation of that day when we will see the myriads of angels, cherubim and seraphim as they serve and make happiness complete for all who have entered God's new creation. *What a hope!* I am so glad I have this hope, an anchor for the soul. With sins *forgiven,* redemption *assured,* salvation a *present possession,* divine nature *within* and this hope *before* us, who would have the least desire to return to the beggarly elements of this world? The hope we have is reserved in God's house for us.

We need not worry or fret about this hope, because Paul tells us that it is laid up for us, and Christ has given His pledge to protect and keep our inheritance "incorruptible, undefiled, that fadeth not away." This was not something new to the believers in the church at Colosse, because Paul said, "of which ye have *already* heard in the word of the truth of the Gospel." Paul preached the pure Gospel, ALL of the Gospel, to those to whom he ministered. There would not be so much backsliding and inconsistent living among believers today if God's preachers would spend more time digging into the deep things of His precious Word, and by so doing feed their parishioners the meat of the Word whereby they would be strengthened and built up in the faith, instead of passing out fifteen-minute sermonettes on

Sunday morning, aimed to please a crowd of shallow church members. With such a hope as Paul describes here, believers would be inspired and encouraged to press on to the mark of the high calling of God in Christ Jesus. With such a hope, they would have no time for things of the world, no time to fellowship with the unfruitful works of darkness and no time for backsliding!

The closing words of verse 5 certainly suggest that the hope laid up in heaven for the believer was a prominent subject with the Apostle Paul. He preached often about the Christian's hope in the Lord Jesus, and the church was well informed concerning it. Paul just *mentions* the hope here, and says to the believers at Colosse, "I need not enlarge upon this message, because bright and glorious as our hope is, you are acquainted with it—you learned about it in the very first days of my preaching the Gospel to you. You *heard* of it, you *received* it, you *possess* this glorious hope." The word of the truth of the Gospel was the only source through which the revealed nature and certainty of our future and celestial blessedness could be learned. Therefore, *Paul preached the word of the truth of the Gospel* to all the churches where God allowed him to minister.

The Christian life is the best life, to be sure. The Christian life is one of expectation and positive enjoyment here on earth; but we look forward to "the hope laid up in heaven." The hope we have goes beyond the dreary wail of the benediction, "Ashes to ashes, dust to dust." The truth of the Gospel throws its radiance and hope beyond the grave. Hallelujah!!

Verse 6: "Which is come unto you, as it is in all the world; and bringeth forth fruit, as it doth also in you, since the day ye heard of it, and knew the grace of God in truth."

The Gospel had been brought to the Colossians and

was now with them, *in their possession* (II Peter 1:4). The statement "as it is *in all the world*" is not confusing if we consider that at that time the world was not inhabited to the extent that it is today. The phrase is used elsewhere by Paul, and simply refers to Judaea and the surrounding areas . . . those countries which to them comprised the world.

The Gospel received by the Colossians was bearing fruit—as certainly it will, for "faith without works is dead." A tree that does not bud is a dead tree; a religionist who bears no fruit is not a believer. All true Christians bear fruit—some thirty, some sixty, some a hundred fold; but nowhere in the Bible does God say, "some brought forth NO fruit!" Every branch that bears not fruit is cut down and consumed. True, born-of-the-Spirit believers will bear fruit—perhaps not an abundance of fruit, but where there is *life*, there is *fruit*.

The Gospel was indeed making progress. The disciples preached the Gospel, people were converted all around them, and their converts in turn became preachers. Therefore, the circle of the Gospel grew larger and larger day by day, as its influence spread (Acts 12:24; 19:20).

". . . Since the day ye heard of (the Gospel) and knew the grace of God in truth." From that very day, the Colossians began to bear spiritual fruit. They bore external fruit, audible fruit—and the grace and love they demonstrated was known and heard about; people became acquainted with true Christianity as demonstrated by the church at Colosse. The Colossians had heard of and knew the grace of God in truth. By hearing the Gospel they had come to know fully the grace of God which is the heart and essence of the Gospel—the message that makes known the glorious fact of the good news that God has in His sovereign grace and favor, pitied and blessed the world and made possible the unmerited salvation that is in Christ Jesus our Lord for all who will come unto God by Him. God had a perfect right to punish the world and destroy mankind; but instead, He provided and made possible redemption through the shed blood of His only begotten Son, the Lord Jesus Christ.

Paul is saying to the Colossians, "Since the day you heard the Gospel of the grace of God, you fully *knew* the grace of God, in truth as in deed. It was the true and complete Gospel of grace that you learned from Epaphras. You heard the true Gospel of grace, you received the true message of grace. The grace of God was taught to you without mutilation or admixture of false philosophy, dogmas, doctrines and traditions of men." However, Paul later gives warning against vain deceit and philosophy, and against men who deviate from the pure grace of our God.

Paul is saying to the Colossians, "Since ye knew the grace of God in truth, you learned the grace of God in its true form without the mixture that is attempting to creep in now—just as you learned it from Epaphras." Epaphras was a true servant of God, untainted with error. He preached pure grace exactly as Paul had taught him:

Verse 7: "As ye also learned of Epaphras our dear fellowservant, who is for you a faithful minister of Christ."

Paul assured the Colossians that the teaching of Epaphras was sealed and sanctioned by divine authority. He was not jealous of this colleague to whom he referred as "our dear fellowservant." Timothy, Paul and Epaphras not only knew and served the same God, but they were closely knit together in the love of God—love for the truth and the preaching of the grace of God. The heart of the Apostle Paul was bound in deep affection to all his fellow-laborers, and he had no animosity toward them, nor sense of rivalry with them. He knew no envy of their success. He was so identified with their ministry and work that whatsoever gladdened them made him happy also. He rejoiced for their victories, and was broken-hearted over their reverses.

The faithfulness of Epaphras was definitely a spiritual asset and benefit to the believers at Colosse. For them, he served faithfully in the Gospel of Christ. This is a brief but noble biography of this servant of God.

Verse 8: "Who also declared unto us your love in the Spirit." Epaphras had brought to Paul the declaration concerning the unusual love of the believers in the Colossian church. He had spoken not only of their love, but had given Paul the news concerning their other spiritual attainments and advancements. However, love is the crown and the essence of all other graces. It was their deep love—first for Christ and the Gospel, then for all saints—that caused the Colossian Christians to produce an abundance of spiritual fruits. When Epaphras declared that the love of the Colossians was "love in the Spirit," he made known the reason for the results in the church at Colosse. A divine change had been brought about in their hearts, and that change had filled them with pure love—the kind of love that only a genuine experience with God can produce. *"He that dwelleth in love, dwelleth in God and God in him."*

In verse 3 Paul declares that as he prayed, he did so from a heart filled with thanksgiving for the Colossian Christians, and he then gives the reason for his thanksgiving. Beginning in verse 9, he makes known the substance of his prayer. He tells the Colossians that he prayed to God on their behalf, asking God to grant unto them blessings fitted for their hearts, their minds, and their daily conduct—that a deeper degree of knowledge might be theirs . . . a higher degree of pure holiness, un-

31

selfishness, usefulness, strength, and blessings provided only by God the Father, and enjoyed only by those who have been translated from the kingdom of darkness into the kingdom of God's dear Son.

PAUL'S SEVENFOLD PRAYER

Verse 9: "For this cause we also, since the day we heard it, do not cease to pray for you, and to desire that ye might be filled with the knowledge of His will in all wisdom and spiritual understanding."

A better translation would read: "On this account, we too, since the day we heard of it, cease not praying and asking . . . ." That is, "Because you know the true grace of God; because you learned true grace *in truth*; because of your faith; because of your love which is demonstrated daily in your conduct and dealings with other saints; because of the blessed hope laid up for you, reserved in heaven, incorruptible, undefiled, protected by Almighty God; because these seal the genuineness of your experience, *we pray continually for you.*"

Paul's special object of supplication is now made known. He prayed, "that ye might be filled with the knowledge of His will in all wisdom and spiritual understanding." (Compare Ephesians 1:17.) Paul desired for the Colossians a complete knowledge of the divine will of God in all its revealed elements and aspects. He wanted them to have perfect, complete knowledge of God's perfect will for them. Every Christian should desire to know God's perfect will for his or her life.

Paul wanted the Colossians to know the divine will of God without any restriction; he wanted them to know God's will in creed and in moral obligation (the one divine basis of what we ought to believe and of what we ought to do as believers), the only rule of true faith and pure Christian manners (I Cor. 1:4–7; I Cor. 2:12; I Cor. 12:8; Eph. 1:17). Paul wanted the believers in Colosse to know the complete, divine will of God in every minute detail, nothing lacking, "in all wisdom and spiritual understanding." If God fills a believer with the knowledge of His divine will, certainly the sphere of the spiritual vision is enlarged. The mind of such a believer is trained and taught in divine things. The spiritual horizon of a believer filled with the knowledge of God's divine will is expanded. The believer whose will is totally and completely surrendered to God gathers spiritual wisdom as he studies and rightly divides the Word of Truth. Spiritual wisdom brings spiritual insight. The birthright of every believer is enjoyment of the Spirit of light in his life. The enjoyment of the Spirit of light is a special privilege, a singular blessing belonging to all believers who will yield unreservedly to God.

When a believer completely yields to the divine will of God and permits God to fill him with the knowledge of His will in all wisdom and spiritual understanding, God then removes the mist which obscures the inner vision of that believer . . . a mist which hinders spiritual understanding and robs the believer of the depth of great spiritual truths and promises laid down in God's holy Word. When a person is completely yielded to God's divine will, God gives to that person a deep love for divine truth and a deep, burning desire for a better understanding of that truth. When the believer is so completely yielded, such surrender enables him to *see through the spiritual eye of understanding*, and thereby receive blessings that the average Christian knows nothing of. Oh, God! Give to us *spiritual understanding!*

Notice the little word, *"all"* . . . "ALL wisdom and ALL spiritual understanding." Wisdom and spiritual understanding are not limited. They may be enjoyed by the

33

surrendered believer to their utmost bounds—and heaven only knows the bounds of God's wisdom and spiritual understanding. "Christ is made unto us wisdom, righteousness, sanctification, and redemption" (I Cor. 1:30).

Not many believers enjoy their spiritual birthright. Most of us accept God's second best—or even His third or fourth best—when we could and should be living in the center of the abundance of God's grace, wisdom, holiness and all spiritual understanding.

Verse 10: "That ye might walk worthy of the Lord unto all pleasing, being fruitful in every good work, and increasing in the knowledge of God." Paul's desire for the believers in the Colossian church was not empty or meaningless. He desired these spiritual blessings *"that ye might walk worthy of the Lord."* To walk worthy of the Lord goes much deeper than the average believer has known. Most believers live a very shallow Christian life. To walk worthy of the Lord is to literally feel the bond of His redeeming blood; to feel the pain He suffered when He shed His blood for the remission of sins. To walk worthy of the Lord is to so love, cherish and worship Him that the very image of Himself is continually before us. To walk worthy of the Lord is to yield to His Spirit and to walk in such harmony *with* the Spirit that we will exhibit His purity, His piety, His humility, His love and His very life. We are to walk in His steps; we are to get into the yoke with Jesus and walk beside Him.

Paul prayed that the Colossians would walk worthy of the Lord *"unto all pleasing."* The highest pleasure of the Lord Jesus is to see Himself—His own likeness—in those who own His Lordship in every phase of their life . . . in their thoughts, in their actions, in their purpose in life, in everything they do. His desire for His children is that we walk worthy of Him, and by so doing secure His approval. "Whether therefore we eat or drink, or whatsoever we do," let us do it all to the glory of God. We should never do anything selfishly nor for vainglory.

In verse 10 Paul prays that the Colossians be "fruitful in every good work, and increasing in the knowledge of God." Spiritual fruit is the first proof of spiritual life within. Spiritual fruits are signified by good works. Read II Corinthians 9:8; II Thessalonians 2:17; Hebrews 13:21; Galatians 5:22; Philippians 1:11. Paul always declared that fruitlessness is deadness. James said, "Faith without works is dead." Jesus said, "By their fruits ye shall know them." A tree with a sapless trunk and a leafless branch is a dead tree.

Paul wanted the Colossians to be "like a tree planted by the rivers of water," a tree covered with foliage, laden and bent low with clusters of goodly, ripened fruit. He wanted them to be trees full of buds bursting forth into blossoms, forming fruit that blessed all with whom they came in contact. He wanted them to be believers interested in and performing every good work . . . *"and increasing in the knowledge of God."* True knowledge of God is the only food that will bring about spiritual growth. A God in shadows, not known in truth, always brings about superstition, doubt and fear. Following such a God leads to fanaticism or mysticism. The more we learn about our God the more we know of His love, His power, His longsuffering, His grace and His majesty. The more we trust Him the more confidence we will have in Him, and the more confidently we will rest our life—past, present and future—in His hands. The more we know of Him the deeper our own experience with Him will be. We will lean upon His arm in the time of need for strength. We will rest upon His bosom and confide in Him in every phase of life. The more we know of Him the more we will love and trust Him, the more we will grow in things spiritual, and the more we will enjoy our spiritual life. If we would walk worthy of our Christ, this fruitbearing and knowledge set forth in verse 10 must be our experience.

Verse 11: "Strengthened with all might, according to His glorious power, unto all patience and longsuffering with joyfulness." This verse describes the spiritual condition in which a believer brings forth fruit. From God comes the power and strength to bring forth fruit. The power to bring forth fruit is *imparted* strength—not strength worked up or brought about through our ability or wisdom—but strength imparted by God, the very power of God Himself within us. Paul clearly refers to the impartation of divine strength and divine power to believers. The natural man is feeble. Fallen humanity is weak, but rises to power when yielded to God's grace, grounded in truth and filled with spiritual understanding.

The branch cannot bear fruit apart from the vine (John 15:1–8). WE cannot bear fruit *apart from the power of God within*. A fruitbearing Christian must be yielded—soul, spirit and body. Our members must be dedicated to Him, instruments of righteousness. We must present our bodies a living sacrifice. The power to be an effective minister is imparted from God Almighty—we do not pray it up, pray it down, work it up, work it down, nor acquire it in a seminary! It comes from Almighty God, and it comes according to His glorious power.

The glory of our God possesses a singular, peculiar might—and it is not just love. God IS love—but also "God is a consuming fire" (Heb. 12:29). Let the believer survey the glory of Almighty God in creation, when He spoke—and the world came into being! Let the believer look at the heavens—the architectural power of God overwhelms us when we gaze at the stars. Look at the mountains, the rivers, the mighty oceans. "The heavens declare the

36

glory of God; and the firmament sheweth His handywork"
(Psalm 19:1). We are amazed by God's power to create.

Consider God in redemption, when His own Son cried
out, "My God, my God! Why hast thou forsaken me?"
The God who spoke this universe into existence could
have spoken one word—and with that word he could have
annihilated every enemy Jesus ever had; but instead, He
turned His head and permitted His Son to die the horrible
death of the cross in order that poor, hell-deserving sinners might be redeemed! Certainly such power amazes
us, even while we are thankful for it. Therefore, if the
spiritual power given to born again believers is fashioned
after the measure of the might of God's glory, then I say
"What power we are armed with, as compared to the power
we know on earth!"

The present generation of preachers and evangelists
who have gone from one college to another, from one
seminary to another, seeking one degree after another,
should stop and turn aside long enough to allow God to
equip and arm them with power to do His work.

A believer—whether minister or layman—equipped with
such power and filled with God to such an extent, will
realize spiritual strength to resist evil, turn his back
upon temptation, banish all fear and doubt, surmount all
obstacles and overcome all difficulties. A believer so
filled with the power of God will find strength to embrace
all opportunities—and, in the end, will obtain victory over
death, hell and the grave! No wonder Paul proclaims in
Colossians 2:10, *"And ye are complete in Him, which is
the head of all principality and power!"*

". . . Unto all patience and longsuffering with joyfulness." We must face the fact that believers in our
present state are not perfect. We live in a tabernacle of
flesh, we have not arrived at our ultimate goal; we are

therefore susceptible to impatience and faithlessness. There is a rest for us, *set before us*—but we have not reached it. Christians are apt to faint when discouragement comes; we are subject to weakness and despondency. Paul prayed for the Colossians (and for all believers) that they would possess the strength of God in order that they might have patience and longsuffering—and *be happy in it.*

The Colossian church was festered with those who taught error, and there might be times when these error-teaching preachers would perplex and confound the Colossians—even some of the most spiritually minded—because they were babes in Christ. Therefore Paul prayed earnestly that they might be strengthened with all might, according to the glorious power of Almighty God . . . strengthened unto all patience and longsuffering with joyfulness. "In quietness and confidence shall be your strength" (Isaiah 30:15).

". . . *With joyfulness.*" The joy of which Paul is speaking here accompanies the graces of longsuffering and patience. The things that come upon us, which demand patience and a longsuffering spirit, should not cause us to be discouraged, despondent, cast down, nor to have a gloomy heart; on the contrary, we should rejoice and be exceedingly glad. We should be joyous when we have opportunity to be tried and tested because of our love for and surrender to pure grace and true Christianity. When we are tried and tested, divine power is given to us in order that we may be *more than conquerors through Him that loved us* (Rom. 8:39). In the Christian experience, even in the darkest hours of trials and heartaches, there are abundant reasons for rejoicing and being exceedingly glad.

Verse 12: "Giving thanks unto the Father, which hath made us meet to be partakers of the inheritance of the saints in light." The normal life for a truly born again believer is to walk worthy, bear fruit, grow in grace, and be strengthened by the power of God in the inner man, in all things giving thanks—for this is the will of God in Christ Jesus.

Paul is here praying for the Colossians that they might walk worthy of the Christ, even in the immediate spiritual battles through which they were passing as error tried to make inroads into the church. Even amidst these difficulties, Paul prayed that they would be strengthened in patience, and that they would rejoice

Believers should always keep in mind that it is Christ who "hath made us able" (II Cor. 3:6), and as we go further into the book of Colossians we will learn that it is *in Christ* that we possess all things. Apart from Him we are nothing, we can do nothing.

It is the Father "who hath made us meet to be partakers of the inheritance of the saints in light." The original language here denotes a portion (a share) which one is to enjoy at the appointed time. The inheritance (allotment) is ours because we have trusted Jesus; in Him we become God's sons, thereby becoming heirs of God and joint heirs with Jesus. The language here has the same meaning as the phrase in Deuteronomy 32:9: "For the Lord's portion is His people; Jacob is the lot of His inheritance." Ephesians 1:11–12 says, "In whom also we have obtained an inheritance, being predestinated according to the purpose of Him who worketh all things after the counsel of His own will, that we should be to the praise of His glory, who first trusted in Christ."

The inheritance here belongs to the saints. The saints are not the Jews, they are not the righteous ones in the Old Testament era. The saints are a specific company—those who belong to Christ because they have trusted Him and are saved upon the merit of His shed blood, having believed in His finished work, having trusted in His saving grace. They are the peculiar company referred to in the epistles as "saints."

"Now therefore ye are no more strangers and foreigners, but fellowcitizens *with the saints*, and of the household of God" (Eph. 2:19).

"That Christ may dwell in your hearts by faith; that ye, being rooted and grounded in love, may be able to comprehend *with all saints* what is the breadth, and length, and depth, and height; and to know the love of Christ, which passeth knowledge, that ye might be filled with all the fulness of God" (Eph. 3:17–19).

Colossians 1:12 closes with "the inheritance of the saints in light." This light, however, is not the light we enjoy here. We walk in the light as He is in the light (I John 1:7). It is true that we enjoy light here in this life, but this *"inheritance in light"* is the future inheritance of the saints. In Ephesians 1:14 the Holy Ghost is called "the EARNEST OF OUR INHERITANCE." In the same chapter, Paul prays that the believers at Ephesus may be able to comprehend the riches of the glory of God's inheritance among His saints. In Acts 20:32, Acts 26:18 and I Peter 1:4 the inheritance is the future glory of the saints. Therefore, we believe Paul is saying here that God has fitted the saints for the future inheritance which is *"the inheritance of the saints in light"* . . . . eternal light.

Heaven is a place of light. We learn in Revelation 21 that there is no need of sun or stars there—the Lamb is the light of the city. The radiance of Him will furnish the light for the city where the saints will live and move throughout eternity. Only saints will dwell in that city—those who are clothed with purity and perfection, nothing short of God's holiness, the righteousness of the Lord Jesus (II Cor. 5:21). No such being exists on this earth in this body. Man is incapable of enjoying the inheritance of light in this body. By nature the natural man is darkness. His mind is darkened, his thoughts are impure, his heart is desperately wicked and must be changed before that man can enter the *kingdom* of light *here*, and inherit the *inheritance* of light at the end of life's journey (John 3:3; I John 1:7).

If unregenerated man should enter heaven, heaven would be hell to him. Heaven is a prepared place for prepared people. The natural man must be changed, because the natural man is not subject to the will of God. No man in the flesh has ever obeyed God's command. There must be a change of heart. Study Adam and Eve; Noah; Abraham; David. Natural man is prone to follow the flesh, and his nature must be brought into harmony with the things of the Spirit. All are born in sin, shapen in iniquity, and "flesh and blood shall not inherit the kingdom of God (the kingdom of light)." But when Jesus comes in the Rapture we will be raised incorruptible. We will have a body of flesh and bone, no blood . . . a body just like Jesus' glorious body (Luke 24; I John 3:1–3). Let me hasten to say that what God commands, God provides and makes possible to the individual. Christ is made unto us wisdom, righteousness, sanctification and redemption. He who knew no sin was made sin that we might be made the righteousness of God in Him. "There is therefore now no condemnation to them who are in Christ Jesus . . . Christ in you, the hope of glory!"

One day, suddenly—"in the twinkling of an eye"— we will pass from pain to rapture, from tears to laughter, from heartaches to jubilant joy beyond human imagination. We will be translated from a world of sorrow to a world of songs, praises and hallelujahs. In this present state, in this earthly body, the inheritance of light is only partially enjoyed. (Heaven begins on earth, and if you are a believer and have not had a taste of heaven, you have been cheated!) But the *fullness* of our inheritance will become ours after the translation of the saints, when we are translated out of this dark world into the perfect day where there is no gloom, no mist . . . only Shekinah glory—the brilliance of light that only the face of Jesus could provide.

Verse 13: "Who hath delivered us from the power of darkness, and hath translated us into the kingdom of His dear Son."

In literal translation the statement reads, "Who rescued us out of the kingdom of darkness." Paul steps directly from the language of prayer and praise into a tremendous theological declaration: God's redeeming love, His unknowable power, translated us out of the kingdom of darkness—the darkness of this world, the darkness of the natural man—into the kingdom of His dear Son, thereby preparing us for the kingdom of light. Jesus said, "I am the Light of the world," but unregenerate man lives in a kingdom of darkness, a kingdom of spiritual gloom, because he lives under the power of Satan, and Satan operates in "works of darkness."

Those who live in the realm of the unbeliever are "children of disobedience and wrath" (Luke 22:53; Acts 26:18).

Ignorance, vice and misery describe the kingdom in which the unbeliever lives. Please notice: In verse 12 we have *the inheritance of the saints in light*, and in verse 13 believers *have been delivered from the power of darkness* (the kingdom of darkness). Thus the kingdom of darkness stands in direct contrast to the inheritance of the saints—the kingdom of light. I repeat: Those who love darkness would not enjoy heaven, and if an unbeliever should accidentally find himself in the center of that Celestial City it would still be hell, because he would be eternally out of place! He could not enjoy one thing there. Heaven is distinctly a prepared place for prepared people, and only those who *are* prepared will enter that city.

Believers are translated into the kingdom of the Son of His love, the only begotten Son of God. Paul refers to Him in verse 13 as *"His dear Son."* The Colossians had been translated out of the realm of darkness; they were at that same moment translated into the kingdom of God's dear Son. They had changed their citizenship and had become citizens of another kingdom, which was a *present possession*, not a future inheritance. (The kingdom of light in its fulness IS a future inheritance, but the translation referred to in verse 13 is a possession here and now!) The split second an unbeliever puts his trust in Jesus, that split second he becomes a member of the kingdom of light. Believers are not immigrants in search of a home; they are not a company of dissatisfied exiles looking for a place to call their own. *Believers are settled in the kingdom of God's dear Son.* We are NOW the sons of God; we are NOW the possessors of eternal life; our citizenship is NOW in heaven. We sit together in heavenly places NOW. We are looking forward to that glorious morning when we will receive our glorified bodies, but our spirits are *already* citizens of the celestial city, the inheritance of light.

Verse 13 closes with the words, "HIS DEAR SON." In the verses that follow, Paul describes the glory of the Saviour, and therefore introduces Him as God's dear Son—the Son of His love. Jesus was the *dearly beloved* Son, God's *only begotten* Son, and God loved Him as only a sovereign God could love a Son. Remember—love is

43

an *attribute*, not an *essence*. Love belongs to *character—* not to *substance*. Love PROMPTS; love does not PRODUCE. God is love, and true love is the radiance of the sun at high noon. Love has the power of a giant stream as it rushes down the mountainside. God's love displayed itself in the radiance of Christ; the *power* of His love displays itself in the miracle evident when a sinner is saved.

Verse 14: "In whom we have redemption through His blood, even the forgiveness of sins." We are members of the kingdom of God's dear Son. We become members of that kingdom through the love of the Father, in the Lord Jesus paying the sin-debt on the cross. We are united to the Son, redeemed through His precious blood— the price He paid that we might enjoy and possess forgiveness of sins. The moment an unbeliever exercises faith in the shed blood of Jesus Christ, the heart is pardoned and forgiven all sin. *Sinners become sons* instantaneously; salvation is a sudden miracle, not a gradual process.

This doctrine was first and foremost in apostolic preaching. Study Acts 5:31, Acts 13:38, Acts 26:18; then compare Exodus 34:7, Isaiah 55:7, Jeremiah 33:8 and Micah 7:18.

The greatest word ever uttered on this earth was the word Jesus spoke when He cried, "*Tetelestai!* (It is finished)"! The blood has been shed, the sin-debt has been paid, redemption has been purchased, paid for in full and brought down to man. Therefore, *we have instant redemption through His blood.* Man's guilt was so deep, the penalty of sin was so tremendous, man's iniquities were so terrible—so utterly hopeless and helpless was man in his natural state, it is no wonder it took the agony, the pain, the misery, the blood of the Lamb of God—the Son of His love! Had not God provided redemption, had He

44

not made possible free and perfect salvation, man would be destined to be damned! Therefore, redemption is not only a great blessing of indescribable grandeur—but redemption is a divine necessity . . . the heart and soul of the Gospel message.

Men have written millions of books about Jesus— His miracles, His methods, and many other subjects concerning the Man and His ministry—but Luke sums it all up in these few words: *"The Son of man came to seek and to save that which was lost"* (Luke 19:10). Jesus Himself declared His mission: "For the Son of man came not to be ministered unto, but to minister, and to give His life a ransom for many" (Matt. 20:28).

He did just that. Jesus came into this world with His eye singled on Calvary. He came to die, to lay His life down, and all hell could not stop Him. Redemption is beyond finite understanding, and we will never fully appreciate it until we see Jesus face to face.

Redemption makes no distinction as having to do with sins . . . it knows no "little sins" or "big sins." Redemption shows no discrimination among transgressors . . . ALL have sinned and come short of the glory of God. Jehovah God laid on Jesus the iniquity of us all, and the loving invitation is, *"Whosoever will*, let him drink of the water of life freely. They that come unto Me, I will in no wise cast out. Come unto Me, all ye that labor and are heavy laden, and I will give you rest." If you close your eyes in sin and open them in hell, it will be because, in the words of Jesus, *"Ye will not come to me, that ye might have life!"* (John 5:40).

Redemption is complete: we have forgiveness from sin, and *every sin* is included. The blood brings freedom from sin and makes us fit for the kingdom of God. Without holiness no man shall see God; *the blood makes us holy.* When we are covered by the blood of Jesus Christ,

45

we are just as holy as the blood that covers us. We are justified by faith in the finished work of the Lamb of God, and to be justified is to be just as just as Jesus is just. Justification is the act of the Sovereign Judge— the great God who gave His Son that redemption might be ours through His blood. Then I ask, *Who shall lay anything to the charge of God's elect? By what authority can redemption be revoked or cancelled?* Please study carefully Romans 8:31–39.

Forgiveness!! How sweet the sound of that word! Forgiveness is more closely connected with the redemption we have in the blood of Jesus than any other blessing provided by the salvation we enjoy in Christ. Forgiveness comes to us in a split second. Many other blessings follow after we have been redeemed, but forgiveness is instant. It is the first blessing—the joy of knowing that forgiveness is ours, guilt is gone, and the burden is lifted! Peace is ours because we are pardoned.

We are commanded to *grow in grace*—and holiness is the product of the Spirit and the Word. As we study the Word, and as the Spirit reveals truth to our hungry hearts, we become stronger, more consecrated—and we enter day by day into a deeper holiness; but in the final analysis, *Christ is our holiness*. The more we know about the Word, the more we trust and appreciate Christ . . . "His dear Son . . . in whom we have redemption . . . who is the image of the invisible God."

Having spoken of Christ and the blessings the believer receives through union with Christ, Paul now lingers on *the name*. All the doctrines taught by Paul, all the truths of his theology, were crystalized around the name of Jesus.

CHRIST EXALTED

Verse 15: "Who is the image of the invisible God,

the firstborn of every creature."

In this verse Paul begins a lofty and comprehensive description of the dignity and rank of the Lord Jesus Christ. He describes God's only begotten Son in phrases of marvelous terseness and harmony. Here, he introduces the *name* of the Son of God, and then in sweeping completeness he introduces the *glory of the person of the Lord Jesus* and His work. There is no doubt that Paul sets forth here the glory and the work of the Lord Jesus, directing it to the believers at Colosse because of the mode of error in that community. The sentences in which Paul describes the dignity, glory, rank and work of Christ remind us of a bursting torrent dashing down the mountainside, sweeping away every barrier that would hinder its speeding on to its destination.

We cannot be dogmatic in defining the error in Colosse, but from all we can learn it seems that Gnosticism was taught there. The teaching of this group denied the actual humanity of Jesus, and also denied His supreme divinity. Because of this, Paul exalts Christ as the one Supreme Creator—not only of this world, but of the entire universe and all that therein is. Paul declares that reconciliation is secured in the body of His flesh, through His cruel death on the cross, through His redeeming blood.

It would seem that in Colosse there was much confusion concerning the spirit-world. The errorists believed that Jesus was superhuman, but they did not fully agree that He was *truly human*. They questioned that He was a man, or fashioned as a man. That there had been a man superior to other men upon the earth, they agreed; but whether this man had blood to shed for the remission of sins, and a soul and body that could be severed in death and reunited in the resurrection power of Almighty God, was doubted—and, by some, was entirely denied. There were many in Colosse who believed in mystical

47

speculation instead of faith in the saving power of Almighty God. Paul declared in words easily understood that Jesus Christ was the God-man; He was divine, yet He was human. He came to purchase redemption through His shed blood; yet Jesus Christ was the image of the invisible God.

In verse 15 Paul is speaking of the Son, the author of redemption and forgiveness of sins. It is, therefore, Jesus Christ our Lord in His mediatorial Person whom Paul characterizes as being "THE IMAGE OF GOD." When He dwelt upon the earth, Jesus Himself said, "He that hath seen Me hath seen the Father." The truth of that statement is simply this: Our only vision of God the Father is in His only begotten Son, the Lord Jesus Christ. "No man knoweth the Father but the Son, and he to whom the Son shall reveal Him." All that we can ever know about God the Father is revealed to us through God the Son. *Christ as Creator and Saviour is the image of God.*

As Redeemer, Jesus is the representative of God on earth. Paul said, "God was in Christ, reconciling the world unto Himself" (II Cor. 5:19). The prophetic name of Jesus was "Emmanuel, *God with us.*" Jesus in His incarnate state brought God so near us as to place Him on earth in a form that we could appreciate, understand, and know. Men saw Him, heard Him and handled Him. They saw in Jesus a weeping, suffering, loving God. Jesus was a living image—not a mystical being, not a spirit from another world—but God in flesh. Jesus while on earth held out to men an image of God in love. He displayed love as no other had ever displayed love on this earth. He was tender, self-denying, kind and long-suffering. No man ever lived or loved or sacrificed as Jesus did.

Those who knew Jesus best knew that He was more than man; His wisdom, His holiness—everything about

Him—testified to that fact. Through stormy elements He came to His disciples—*walking upon the waves*. When the dead were recalled from the grave . . . when, touched with His tender hands, death gave way to life, those who witnessed knew they were standing in the presence of divinity. When He rebuked the storm with "Peace! Be still!" the wind grew calm, the boisterous waves settled around the prow of the little ship—and the disciples knew they had heard the voice of God! They knew they were in the presence of Jehovah, who said, "I KILL, AND I MAKE ALIVE; I WOUND, AND I HEAL" (Deut. 32:39).

When five thousand hungry people watched Him break the loaves and fishes to feed the multitude (with much to spare), they knew the food they ate had been touched by hands that were more than the hands of man; the hands of God had broken the loaves and fishes.

His hands touched and healed the leper, thus disobeying all the laws of medicine and all the social laws of that day. His hands touched blinded eyes and gave them sight . . . the hands of Him who came to give men life abundantly. The wonderful words He uttered arrested the hearts of His enemies and in John 7:44–46, when the officers were asked why they did not bring Him, they simply answered, "Never man spake like this man!" His daily miracles testified to His divinity. Everything He did and said demonstrated divine omniscience and omnipotence.

I am talking about God's only begotten Son . . . the Son of His love . . . the Son who walked on this earth, a *visible image* of the *invisible God*.

Verse 15 closes with the statement, "*the firstborn of every creature.*" The meaning of these words is simply this: "Firstborn in reference to the whole creation." The firstborn was a father's representative in all things and acted in his father's name. Christ stands as the firstborn of God the Father, and all transactions between God the Father and man must be transacted with Christ. The only way we can approach our sovereign God is through the Son, the Lord Jesus.

God the Father is invisible: *"No man hath seen God at any time."* Jesus said, "God is a Spirit, and they that worship Him must worship Him in spirit and in truth." The sovereign God—omnipotent, omniscient and omnipresent—is invisible, but the universe was not left without a God who could be seen: *Jesus wrapped God up in flesh, brought Him down to man*, and presented Him to man in a body—*the very image of the invisible God.*

"The earth is the Lord's, and the fulness thereof; the world and they that dwell therein" (Psalm 24:1). This earth exists as a result of God the Son: "All things were made by Him; and without Him was not any thing made that was made" (John 1:3). Hebrews 1:1–3 is very enlightening concerning the creation of this universe. All things were created by Jesus, He arranged all things, He supervises all things, all things belong to Him.

All creation was created by Him and for Him. He is creation's firstborn. He is the Chief and the Governor, the Ruler and Controller of all creation. The devil has no power except the limited power that Jesus allows. When Pilate boasted, "Speakest thou not unto me? knowest thou not that I have power to crucify thee, and have power to release thee?" Jesus replied, "Thou couldest have no power at all . . . *except it were given thee from (my Father)*" (John 19:10,11).

In the days of the Old Testament, the firstborn inherited peculiar rights and privileges, and all management was entrusted to him. *Jesus is the firstborn of the whole creation*, He is the Governor of all creation, the

Lord of all creation—and He brought down to this universe the image, the attributes and the unknowable mercy of the unseen Jehovah God.

Yes, in spite of the modernists and liberals—and all the other haters of God and deniers of the Bible—Jesus is the firstborn of every creature. God's love to Him has given Him this glorious pre-eminence, this double portion: "THOU ART MY SON, THIS DAY HAVE I BEGOTTEN THEE!" Here is plainly implied that Christ existed before all creatures, for He has never stood in any other (secondary) relation to the universe.

When Jesus was baptized, God the Father said in an audible voice, "This is my beloved Son, in whom I am well pleased" (Matt. 3:17). Again, on the Mount of Transfiguration, when Peter, James and John witnessed the transfigured Christ, a bright cloud overshadowed them and God's voice out of the cloud said, "This is my beloved Son, in whom I am well pleased; hear ye Him" (Matt. 17:5).

Just before Jesus went to the cross, He cried out in agony of soul and spirit, "What shall I say? Father, save me from this hour: but for this cause came I unto this hour. Father, glorify thy name. *Then came there a voice from heaven, saying, I have both glorified it, and will glorify it again.* The people therefore, that stood by, and heard it, said that it thundered: others said, An angel spake to Him. Jesus answered and said, This voice came not because of me, but for your sakes. Now is the judgment of this world: now shall the prince of this world be cast out. And I, if I be lifted up from the earth, will draw all men unto me" (John 12:27–32).

Jesus was the Architect when the mansions were built in the Father's house: "Let not your heart be troubled: ye believe in God, believe also in me. In my

51

Father's house are many mansions: if it were not so, I would have told you. *I go to prepare a place for you.* And if I go and prepare a place for you, I will come again, and receive you unto myself; that where I am, there ye may be also" (John 14:1–3).

Jesus was "the firstborn of every creature." Truly He existed before all creatures, even before the mansions in the Father's house and before the foundation of the world was laid. *Jesus was with the Father in the beginning.*

Verse 16: "For by Him were all things created, that are in heaven, and that are in earth, visible and invisible, whether they be thrones, or dominions, or principalities, or powers: all things were created by Him, and for Him."

Certainly creation is here, in the fullest and most unqualified sense, ascribed to the Lord Jesus Christ. This doctrine is in perfect harmony with the theology of John the Beloved (John 1:3). Mark this in your heart and mind, beloved: That which *had no being* before, *was brought into being* by the Lord Jesus Christ. There was no universe until Jesus commanded it to be. He spoke— and it was done. Every form of matter and life, regardless of what that form may be, owes its origin and existence to the Son of God. No matter in what sphere life or atoms may be found, nor in what quantities or qualities, in heaven or in earth, *all was created*, all had its origin, *in Christ.* The creative action of the Lord Jesus Christ had no limited bounds. "In the beginning God created the heaven and the earth" (Gen. 1:1).

It is difficult for the finite mind to grasp this; but read it, re-read it, and *believe* it—because it is true: Every kind of matter—complex or simple; planet, star or atom; giant sun or little clod in the field; every blade of grass, every giant redwood in the forest; every species

52

of life from worm to angel, from bug to cherubim; every fish in the sea, every fowl in the air; every insect, every order of intellect—whether it be that of man or beast; every being *around* us, *above* us, *beneath* us; the splendor of the mansions in the Father's house, and the hillsides of earth with streams and beautiful flowers in the meadow, are the product of *"the Firstborn of every creature."* For by Him were all things created—and when God says "all things," He means ALL THINGS . . . all things in heaven, all things in earth, all things visible or invisible. ALL CREATION owes its origin to the Son of God!

The men who study the stars tell us that the further they penetrate into outer space, the more giant stars they find. New worlds of stars—myriads of them—can be seen each time the telescope becomes a little more powerful.

It may be that Paul was thinking of *heaven proper* when he referred to "things invisible," for he adds, "whether they be *thrones*, or *dominions*, or *principalities*, or *powers*." Paul's desire was to show that Jesus is the Creator—not just of lower life and things upon the earth (things visible), but that He is also the Creator of higher beings—even in regions invisible to the human eye. No atom is too minute, no creature too gigantic, for His creative power.

Verse 16 closes with the words, *"All things were created by Him and for Him."* We clearly see from this statement that the act of creation originally was totally and entirely in Christ. The completion was in Him, and in Him alone. With no help whatsoever, *Christ created.* He was not simply *instrumental* in creating all things; but He is the *cause* of creation. Without Him there could have been no creation. The very impulse to create came upon Him from within—by His own power . . . power of which He was the Originator. All things were created

IN Him and BY Him. Source, motive, desire, energy . . .
ALL were in Jesus. He was not a contractor working
out the plans drawn up by an architect. *He designed His
own creation and executed His own enterprise.* He thought
it all, wrought it all—nor did He ask for assistance in
the erection. He did not ask anyone to help Him find
space, lay the foundation, or furnish the fabric. He created the earth and all that therein is. He created the
heavens and all that therein is. By His hand He made
ALL things. Regardless of what has happened to this
earth and to all creation in the past, regardless of what
will happen in the future, the fact remains that all things
were created "BY Him and FOR Him." Those words
make known His FINAL PURPOSE in all creation.

God could not permit any creature, apart from the
Son of His love, to possess such power or enjoy such
privilege. Only Jesus could be the One "OF WHOM,
TO WHOM, AND FOR WHOM ARE ALL THINGS!" No
one but Jesus could have such freedom of action and
privilege in Himself and for Himself. Any other creature
with such freedom would surprise heaven and astonish
all hell!

"In the beginning, God . . . ."—God the Father, Son,
and Holy Ghost. Had God remained alone, His glory
would have remained unseen and His praises would have
been unsung. God longed to impart His happiness and
His glory to creatures fitted to enjoy and possess that
happiness and glory. Therefore, Christ created all things
for Himself in order that He, according to His eternal
blueprint, might exhibit His glory in creatures fashioned
by the grace of God—creatures spotless, without blame,
holy and presentable to God. IT IS IN THIS CREATOR,
the Lord Jesus Christ, that "we have redemption, the
forgiveness of sins." Certainly redemption is the no-
blest and most sublime of all His works.

Since the Scriptures teach us that all things were created "for Him," we know that what has been *created* is still being *preserved*. All things were brought together by Him and are *being held together* in Him. It is the arm of Christ the Creator that upholds this universe, and if He were to withdraw His mighty arm all things would fade into original non-existence. Before Jesus created all things, *there were no "all things."* God's great created empire depends upon Him in every minute detail. Turn your eyes to the blazing sun, 93,000,000 miles away: Who keeps pouring fuel on that gigantic fire? When the full moon shines and the nights are bright, gaze upon that beauty: Who guides the moon and the planets as they journey through space? Whose master-hand prevents a colossal catastrophe? All the functions of nature are governed by the One who created all things by Himself, in Himself and for Himself—God the Son, our Redeemer. Thus the universal balance is preserved. Each tree yields fruit after its kind, according to the original edict of Jehovah God. Evening and morning still alternate, as declared in the beginning. Creations innumerable in the great wide oceans look up to the Creator. He sees all, He provides for all—*and to Him we owe our all!*

Do you not stand amazed that such a Creator left the Father's bosom and became our Redeemer by way of the cross? Does not such love cause you to bow your head in deep humility and thank God in a prayer of worship, adoration and thanksgiving *that God so loved?* (I am speaking of the God in the first chapter of Genesis— the God who spoke, *and the world was* . . . the same God whom we find as a babe in a manger in the first chapter of Matthew.) I am speaking of the God whom Isaiah calls *the Lord God*—Creator of the ends of the earth, "who hath measured the waters in the hollow of His hand, and meted out heaven with the span" (Isaiah 40:12a). This is the same God whom we find on a cross in the Gospels. The God Jeremiah calls "the true God, the living God, and the everlasting King" is the same God who, in John 1:14, was made flesh and dwelt among us. Jeremiah's God, the everlasting King, is the same God who wept over Jerusalem; the same God who wiped tears from His eyes at the tomb of the beloved Lazarus; the same God who girded Himself with a towel and washed the dusty, tired feet of His disciples. The God of the Old Testament, crowned with honor, glory and majesty, is the same God who was crowned with thorns and nailed in nakedness to a cross, to be gazed upon by multitudes who mocked as they passed by. The God Ezekiel saw sitting on a throne of sapphire with a rainbow about His head and cherubim all around Him, is the same God who in John 19 hangs bleeding on a cross while soldiers divide His belongings and gamble for His coat!

Yes, the God who created all things "had not where to lay His head" while on earth. He left *all*, He came to *nothing*. He took a body—He suffered, bled and died— that you and I might be saved. I confess it is impossible for me to understand all about it. It is beyond my imagination. *Why should He love me so?* Why should He leave the ivory palaces and come to this earth to be beaten, scorned, spit upon, stripped and nailed to a cross, pierced with a spear—and *buried in a borrowed tomb*? Why should He do all of that for *me*? for *you*? The answer is found in the Scriptures, though I confess I do not fully understand what I now quote:

"But God, who is rich in mercy, for His great love wherewith He loved us, even when we were dead in sins, hath quickened us together with Christ, (by grace ye are saved;) And hath raised us up together, and made us sit together in heavenly places in Christ Jesus: THAT IN THE AGES TO COME HE MIGHT SHEW THE EXCEED-

ING RICHES OF HIS GRACE IN HIS KINDNESS TO-
WARD US THROUGH CHRIST JESUS" (Eph. 2:4–7).
. . . "EVEN AS GOD FOR CHRIST'S SAKE HATH FOR-
GIVEN YOU" (Eph. 4:32). God permitted Jesus to come
to earth, and Jesus willingly came. He paid sin's debt
that we poor, hell-deserving sinners who believe on Him
unto salvation, may demonstrate to all God's creation
the exceeding glory, riches and power of His saving
grace. God will put the New Testament Church, the
Bride of Christ, on display in the Pearly White City sus-
pended between heaven and earth, and the light of that
city will illumine all things made new throughout the
ceaseless ages of eternity.

Verse 17: "And He is before all things, and by Him
all things consist." This verse in reality is an "Amen"
to all that has been said in verses 15 and 16. Jesus
WAS before anything else—He was in the beginning with
the Father. He is not inferior to the Father, nor has He
ever been. By Him all things consist, and if it were
possible for anything to happen to Jesus, all things would
immediately become NONexistent. All the space now
occupied by earth and planets would be empty blackness.
He is the Creator of all things . . . in earth, in heaven,
under the earth . . . *all things*; and all things are dependent upon Him for their continued existence.

Verse 18: "And He is the head of the body, the
Church: who is the beginning, the firstborn from the
dead; that in all things He might have the pre-eminence."

"And He is the head of the body—THE CHURCH."
Paul now begins to give the relationship between Christ
and the Church. Christ stands out as the Supreme Head—
the one supreme Guardian, the one Saviour, the one Governor, the All-in-All . . . *Christ and none other*! "The
Church" in verse 18 does not refer to the local assembly,
but to the redeemed body of faithful sons of God—those

who have salvation through His precious blood. In the previous verses Paul has shown Jesus Christ to *be* the Head of the Church: He is *the image of God,* and is therefore divine. He is *supreme in the universe*—He created it, and it continues to exist because of His power. He created all things, supports all things, and without Him all things would become nonexistent. One so highly exalted is plainly capable of being the Head of the Church, which is composed of the saints of God. He is the God and Saviour of all believers. He is their Protector, the object of their worship and the One who blesses the believer. "Every good gift and every perfect gift is from above"—from God (James 1:17a).

We see here that both the Church and the universe are under one divine administration. He who is King of kings and Lord of lords—King of the earth and all creation—is the Head of the true Church. He has a right to be: *He holds that position through the merit of His shed blood* (Eph. 5:25).

". . . Who is the beginning. . . ." This is practically the same statement we find in Revelation 3:14, and means the same thing. Christ stands alone in solitary grandeur and glory as the singular source of all blessings and honor described in the preceding verses and throughout the New Testament. "He is the head of the body, the Church." He is the one source of the existence of the Church and its blessings. He is "the first begotten from the dead," and He is the reconciler of men to Jehovah God by the blood of His cross. Christ is the initial source of existence and blessings. Before Christ, there was nothing. Because of Him, all things exist and will continue to exist. Through His divine love and gracious grace, the Church came into existence. Without Him salvation could never have been. Therefore, since He ransomed the Church, does He not have a right to rule as its Head?

Christ is the author of blessing, regardless of the kind or amount of blessings enjoyed. We sing about "showers of blessings," we read about "wells of living water" and "springs of eternal life." All this is true— but it is Jesus who supplies the showers of blessings, the water in the well of eternal life, and the rain that fills the springs of salvation. Christ is, in the most un-limited sense, "THE BEGINNING."

Not only is Jesus the Head of the Church and the beginning of all things, but He is *"the firstborn from the dead."* (The literal translation should read, "the first *begotten* from the dead.") The wages of sin is death: when sin is finished, it brings forth death. All have sinned; therefore, *in Adam all die.* Jesus (the second Adam) became "the first begotten from the dead"— not that He simply died and rose again, but that He be-came the Conqueror of death, hell and the grave.

Because of Him, the dead in Christ will rise again. He destroyed "him that hath the power of death" (Heb. 2:9,14,15). When He was "cut off, but not for Himself," not only did He "finish transgression and make an end of sin," but He also "abolished death."

Our Christ, our Redeemer, now has in His possession the keys of death and hell. One glorious day the Lord Jesus will descend into the atmospheric heavens above us. He will give a great shout, the voice of the archangel and the trump of God will sound, and those who have died in Christ will awake—not one will be lost; earth and sea will give up every occupant who died in the Lord. The bodies will be raised incorruptible, the spirit will reunite with the glorified body and be caught up in beauty, to be with Him in the air. These vile bodies will then be fashioned like unto His own glorious body.

Verse 18 closes with the words, ". . . That in all things He might have the pre-eminence." This statement indicates—*not the result*—but *God's final purpose* of His entire economy, that Christ may show Himself first IN ALL THINGS. Paul means simply this: Because Christ is everything he has described Him to be, He has all things in His power. He stands first in relation to the universe, for He is its visible God. He is the Creator and the Preserver of the universe. He is the head and the protector of the Church. He is "the resurrection and the life." As the image of the invisible God, the great Eternal Spirit, Jesus has the pre-eminence. Christ is without date of origin, and He is eternal . . . He can never die. Christ is able to do exceeding abundantly *above anything we ask or think*. His power knows no limit of operation. His wealth—both spiritual and natural—is inexhaustible. His mind comprises all probabilities. He has already made the decision concerning all certainties. He shares equal power, glory and honor with the Father and the Holy Ghost.

As the image of the *invisible* God, Christ has the pre-eminence—*Christ has visibility*; the Father and the Spirit are *not* visible. Christ is the visible God whom men saw, touched, handled, with whom they ate and whom they recognized after His resurrection. Today He sits, in a body, at the right hand of God the Father. There is a MAN in heaven—a man of flesh and bone (no blood . . . He gave His blood for the sin of the world). "There is one God, and one mediator between God and men, the man Christ Jesus" (I Tim. 2:5).

Please note: "the MAN" . . . not an angel or a spirit, but the MAN Christ Jesus. NOW OUR LORD JESUS CHRIST IS THE MOST GLORIOUS BEING IN ALL OF GOD'S CREATION . . . either heaven or earth. Proof? "When the Son of man shall come in His glory, and all the holy angels with Him, then shall He sit upon the throne of His glory" (Matt. 25:31). "Father, I will that they also, whom thou hast given me, be with me where I am; *that they may behold my glory*, which thou hast given me: for thou lovedst me before the foundation of the world" (John 17:24).

Because of His complete obedience to Jehovah God, the eternal Spirit; because He satisfied Jehovah God in every detail and fulfilled every jot and tittle of the Law; because He was able to look God in the face and say, "It is finished," Christ has been exalted to the highest position possible, as befits the most glorious Being in heaven and in earth.

The incarnation of Jesus illuminates every Old Testament prophecy concerning Himself and the promise of His coming. In the New Testament the incarnation is clearly set forth as FACT! When Jesus left the Father's bosom and came to this earth in human form, the human did not dwarf the divine . . . He was God in flesh. When He laid His life down and was buried and rose again, the divine did not absorb the human. Both human and divine coexist without confusion or mixture. Jesus is the God-Man. He battled all hell, all evil spirits of the underworld, all demon monstrosities—and conquered them all, as we will learn in chapter two. Through His victory in battle, His shed blood on the cruel cross, He won for Himself the grand and glorious position as Head of all things in heaven and in earth.

Saving faith decides on Christ, and Christ alone . . . not Christ AND!—but CHRIST!!! He is our all-sufficiency, and we are complete in Him. True love has CHRIST for its one and only motto. True faith and true salvation bring to the heart of the believer a love for Christ that can say, "None other but Jesus! I love Him with my whole soul, spirit, mind and strength!"

Verse 19: "For it pleased the Father that in Him should all fulness dwell." This verse is a continuation of the thought that closes verse 18: ". . . that in all things He might have the preeminence"; and in order for this to be possible it was imperative that God the Father be pleased with Jesus to the extent that God bestowed upon Him all fulness, even fulness that only God could produce. It was God's pleasure that all fulness dwell in His beloved Son—the Son of God's love, the Son of whom God said, "I am well pleased."

Whatever is needed to save a world of chaos and restore perfect harmony to a disrupted universe, is treasured up in the Lord Jesus Christ. Whatever the believer needs from the moment of redemption to the moment when we stand in His presence—whether it be knowledge, faith, purity, hope, comfort, strength, pardon, or life—we find in His inexhaustible abundance. In Christ all fullness dwells. *In Him* there is an abundance of anything and everything the believer needs.

Jesus was God in flesh; He was the Word made flesh; but a message of provision that is not applicable would be inadequate. Not only has *ample provision* been made through the finished work of the Lord Jesus Christ; not only has salvation for the sinner been purchased through His shed blood; but *the purchased salvation has been placed within the reach of every poor lost sinner who will come to God by Christ.*

Jesus said, "And I, if I be lifted up from the earth, will draw all men unto me." He WAS lifted up—and every unbeliever who will turn sin-blinded eyes toward the cross will receive the *opening* of his blinded eyes (II Cor. 4:3,4). The unbeliever's vision will be clear when he sees the bleeding Lamb . . . when he sees the atoning blood that was shed for the remission of sin. And when the mind that has been "blinded by the god of this age" realizes that the Lamb hung on that tree for each and every sinner, faith will then bring salvation, purify the soul, and assure an eternal inheritance. We are not only saved by grace through faith, realizing that the Gospel is the power of God unto salvation to everyone who believeth—but the believer who exercises faith in the blood of the Lamb slain for the remission of sin will realize that in the shed blood we not only have redemption, but we also are *"kept by the power of God through faith."*

In Jesus, the believer finds every grace—*as* needed, *when* needed, *under all conditions.* The invitation is simply "Come unto Me." And all who are tormented in the pit of the damned will beg for mercy because "Ye would not come to Me, that ye might have life!"

Paul said, "My God shall supply all your need according to His riches in glory by Christ Jesus." Therefore, every blessing needed—in sickness or in health; in trial or in duty; for body or for soul; in life or in death; for earth or for heaven; for time or for eternity—is found in the fullness of Him whom it pleased the Father that "in Him should all fullness dwell."

THE RECONCILING WORK OF CHRIST

Verse 20: "And, having made peace through the blood of His cross, by Him to reconcile all things unto Himself; by Him, I say, whether they be things in earth, or things in heaven."

The opening statement in this verse is tremendous: *"Having made peace* through the blood of His cross." Peace! How sweet the word! The night Jesus was born, the angels proclaimed "Peace on earth, good will toward men." We have never known that wonderful state on earth among men, but *we will know it* in the new earth when Jesus sits on the throne in Jerusalem and the knowledge of the Lord covers the earth as the waters now cover the sea.

Just before His ascension, Jesus said to His disciples, "Peace I leave with you, my peace I give unto you: not as the world giveth, give I unto you. Let not your heart be troubled, neither let it be afraid" (John 14:27). It was the Lord "who filleth all in all" who spoke those words. The peace Jesus purchased at the tremendous price of His blood certainly applies to the individual—the sinner saved by grace; but it goes much deeper and reaches much, much further than the redemption of the individual. When we study the Word of God and search the Scriptures, we need not wonder at the far-reaching results, yea, *the infinite results*—of the death of the Lord Jesus Christ.

Do you know who it was who died on the cross that day on Golgotha? Can you realize that the One on the cross was the Creator . . . the Preserver . . . the beginning and the end of all things? Creation in its fullest extent and in its farthest reach will be affected by His death. Jesus laid aside the splendor of the Godhead, to take a body and walk in the flesh of man upon this earth. He died in and for a world He created, to satisfy divine justice and glorify the Father whom He loved—the Father who sent Him and surrendered Him to pay sin's debt. No wonder the death of this Person should be felt everywhere—to the ends of the earth and to the highest heaven!

Before the foundation of the world, it was agreed between Father, Son and Holy Ghost that Jesus would redeem, by His shed blood, all who would come unto God by Him. Not only man, created in the image of God, but "*the whole creation* groaneth and travaileth in pain together until now" (Rom. 8:22 ff). These verses tell us that all creation is waiting for that glorious day when Jesus will return to this earth to deliver it from the curse, and to give to His redeemed ones bodies like unto His own glorious body. Therefore, the sufferings of this present time are not worthy to be compared to the glory that will be revealed in us (Rom. 8:18).

Not only will we share in the glory, but all creation will be delivered from the curse. It will be a glorious day when Jesus comes back to finish redemption's plan. It is true that the soul is redeemed now—yes; but the body will be changed when He comes in the Rapture and the first resurrection takes place. All creation will be delivered when the sons of God are manifested in His glorious second coming. The death of Jesus was a divine MUST—there was no other way. Therefore, He *has made* peace "through the blood of His cross," for all who believe on Him and trust Him as Saviour. He *will make peace* "through the blood of His cross" for all creation when He comes in that glorious day.

In this day of bloodless preaching and bloodless religion, it is still The Blood (the blood of His cross) that brings peace and salvation. *"Without the shedding of blood is no remission"* (Heb. 9:22). *"The blood of Jesus Christ, God's Son, cleanseth us from all sin"* (I John 1:7). The paramount difference between Christianity and pagan religions is that Christianity has a God who SHED His blood in love for a lost world, while the pagan gods are continually *calling for blood* . . . the blood of the people who worship a dead stone god that cannot see, hear, nor speak. Our God gave His own blood—once, for all, forever, never to be repeated; but the poor heathen returns again and again and again with blood, blood and more blood!

When the Bible speaks of the blood of Jesus, it is always speaking of the atoning sacrifice *of* Himself, presented willingly *by* Himself on Calvary. When blood is shed on earth between fellowmen, a feud is created

65

that only results in the shedding of more blood. When man sheds the blood of his fellowman, many times friends or relatives of the slain man avenge his death by retaliation in bloodshed. *Jesus* died the most shameful death any man could die in His day . . . a death that was violent as well as vicarious; but HIS death brings peace and quietness, and restores alliance where there has been enmity. His death heals the breach between heaven and earth.

Never man died like Jesus died. He willingly laid His life down—no man took it from Him. No man murdered Jesus, though it is true that men nailed Him to the cross. Jesus cleared up that matter when He said, "No man taketh (my life) from me, but I lay it down of myself. I have power to lay it down, and I have the power to take it again. This commandment have I received of my Father" (John 10:18).

In the Garden of Eden, peace was broken between God and man when Adam deliberately disobeyed God, although God had plainly told him that the day he ate of the forbidden fruit he would die. Adam disobeyed God— and peace and fellowship were broken. God was offended. He sought out Adam, condemned his fig-leaf covering and provided His own blood-bought covering. He rejected Adam's excuses and put all creation under a curse.

He who died on Calvary's hill . . . the One who hung on the old rugged cross . . . possessed *God's nature*— the nature of the offended One; but He also possessed *man's* nature—the nature of the *offending one.* And because He possessed the nature of God (who had been offended) and the nature of man (who offended God), He was qualified to settle the offence and mediate *between* God and man. Therefore the blood of Jesus could be poured out as a peace offering—and that is exactly what happened on Calvary. Just before Jesus died, He said to the heavenly Father, "IT IS FINISHED!" In His own words, He came to fulfill the Law and the prophets (Matt. 5:17). In the shed blood of Jesus the holy Law of God is satisfied. Because of that satisfaction, guilty, hell-deserving sinners are set free from the curse, and thus God reconciles the world unto Himself. Man, having been justified by faith in the shed blood of Jesus Christ, is at peace with God. "THEREFORE being justified by faith, we have peace with God through our Lord Jesus Christ: By whom also we have access by faith into this grace wherein we stand, and rejoice in hope of the glory of God" (Rom. 5:1,2). The Saviour of whom Paul preached was not just a creature—He was *Creator*—He was the beginning and the ending of all things.

Verse 21: "And you, that were sometime alienated and enemies in your mind by wicked works, yet now hath He reconciled."

Paul speaks directly to the Colossians in this verse. He does not disguise the truth when he describes to them their past condition of spiritual alienation from God, which is the character of the heathen world to which the Colossians belonged. He went further, to tell them that they were not only *aliens*, but that in their minds they were *enemies* toward God, practicing wicked works. Before conversion the Colossians had held enmity against God in their minds, hating Him because of a corrupt mind. "If our Gospel be hid, it is hid to them who are lost, in whom the god of this age hath blinded the minds of them . . ." (II Cor. 4:3,4). A person must *think* right *about* God before he can *pray* right *to* God, claiming mercy through the shed blood of Jesus.

Paul is saying to the Colossians, "Think of it! It is wonderful! It pleased God that in Christ should all fulness dwell, and that He should reconcile all things to Himself. And even YOU (once aliens and enemies, but now reconciled), it pleased Him to present holy and perfect before Him."

Man does not win his way back to a holy God by winning God's favor through offerings or sacrifices. Yea—though we "give our bodies to be burned and have not love, it profiteth nothing." The only way man can return to God is through the reconciliation purchased by the blood of Jesus on the cross.

Verse 22: "In the body of His flesh through death, to present you holy and unblameable and unreproveable in His sight."

This verse is a continuation of the preceding one. Paul had dwelt at length on the dignity and majesty of Jesus, but here he speaks of His incarnation. In Jesus was a union of extremes—a union of God and man, of earth and heaven. Christ was God, and He was man. He was in earth, yet He came directly from heaven. God Almighty was His Father through the Holy Ghost overshadowing the Virgin Mary (Luke 1:26—33). "IN THE BODY OF HIS (CHRIST'S) FLESH THROUGH DEATH." Reconciliation is in His body, and had not Jesus taken a body of flesh He could never have brought about reconciliation between God and man.

There were teachers in the Colossian area who refused to accept the fact that Jesus Christ was man in flesh, that He died the death of all men in flesh; but it is a Bible fact that the body of Jesus was a genuine physical body, and it was in the body of His flesh that He made reconciliation possible. He literally died—and *by His death* peace was made possible between God and man. It is impossible for God to die (Psalm 90:1,2); God is an eternal Spirit (John 4:24); He had no beginning, He will have no ending; He has always been, He always will be. Jesus was *God in flesh*, and without the *flesh*

68

there could have been no *death*. Without His *death*, there could have been no *reconciliation*. Without reconciliation God and man could never have come together. But through the blood of Jesus Christ we are reconciled to God, and hid with Christ IN God (Col. 3:3). One day we will stand before God in all of His holiness, Jesus will confess that we are His—and we will be accepted by the Father *"for Christ's sake."*

The last part of verse 22 tells us the purpose of reconciliation: ". . . to present you holy and unblameable and unreproveable in His sight." Earlier in the series I made the statement, "What God demands, God provides," and that is true. The presentation mentioned here is not on earth, but at the consummation of all things— the final acceptance before the throne of His holiness when the saints shall have come to maturity, when they have been crowned and perfected (Eph. 5:27). We will stand before God . . . spotless, blameless, without wrinkle . . . holy, pure, untouched by sin.

We stand before God accepted—but *only in the beloved.* The only possible way man can approach God is in Christ. In Christ is the only possible way we can ever hear Him say, "Well done." The only possible way we can enter the Father's house is in Christ. "I am the Way, the Truth, and the Life. No man cometh unto the Father, but by me" (John 14:6). "I am the Door: by me if any man enter in, he shall be saved" (John 10:9).

Verse 23: "If ye continue in the faith grounded and settled, and be not moved away from the hope of the Gospel, which ye have heard, and which was preached to every creature which is under heaven; whereof I Paul am made a minister." The truth set forth in this verse is the attainment of spiritual perfection and the honor of presentation to God. There will be those who will stand before God ashamed and in dishonor. Do we have any Scripture to substantiate such a statement? Indeed we do!

"And now, LITTLE CHILDREN, abide in Him; that, when He shall appear, we may have confidence, and not be ashamed before Him at His coming" (I John 2:28). According to that Scripture, there will be Christians ashamed when they stand before God.

"But ye, beloved (sons of God), BUILDING UP YOURSELVES ON YOUR MOST HOLY FAITH, praying in the Holy Ghost, keep yourselves in the love of God, looking for the mercy of our Lord Jesus Christ unto eternal life. And of some have compassion, making a difference: and others save with fear, pulling them out of the fire; hating even the garment spotted by the flesh" (Jude 20–23).

Christians are here admonished to build themselves on "most holy faith," praying, keeping themselves in love, looking for the mercy of our Lord Jesus unto eternal life. Paul refers to those who will be literally pulled out of the fire, their garments spotted by the flesh.

In I Corinthians 3:11–15 Paul describes believers who will witness the burning of their works: "If any man's work shall be burned, he shall suffer loss: but he himself shall be saved; yet so as by fire." Read and study that passage very carefully. There will be children of God who will suffer loss. Their works will be burned, but they will be saved—the *spirit* will be saved, *stewardship* will be burned.

John warns us to be careful, be alert, in order that we *"lose not those things which we have wrought, but that we receive a full reward"* (II John 8). The preceding and following verses set forth the reason why John gives this admonition: "Many deceivers are entered into the world, who confess not that Jesus Christ is come in the

70

flesh. This is a deceiver and an antichrist." John tells us that if anyone abide not in the doctrine of Christ, he has not Christ; but if he abide in the doctrine of Christ, he has both Father and Son. Then John says, "If there come any unto you, and bring not this doctrine, receive him not into your house, neither bid him God speed: For he that biddeth him God speed is partaker of his evil deeds" (II John 10,11).

Such admonition would be classed as rank heresy today! If such a sermon were preached from some pulpits in our modern churches, the minister who preached that sermon would be asked to resign. The common doctrine today is "the Fatherhood of God, the brotherhood of man, everyone is good, no one is bad." But that is not what the Bible says. There was a group whom John refused to baptize. He said they looked more like snakes than like sheep—a self-righteous group who claimed to be sons of Abraham. That same group said to Jesus, "We be sons of Abraham, and have never been in bondage." But Jesus said, "You are mistaken. I will tell you who you are: *Ye are of your father, the devil!*" (John 8:44). As believers, we need to be very careful. We need to continue in the faith, we need to be grounded, immovable and stedfast as the Rock of Gibraltar concerning the Gospel.

The statement "If ye continue in faith" does not suggest doubt, or that the Colossians may fall away from the faith. That is not the meaning at all. (Note Romans 6:1 and Ephesians 3:18.) Paul is not teaching the Colossians that *salvation* depends upon *continuance in faith.* The truly born again, blood-washed believer *will continue* in faith. The blessings of true salvation through the blood of Jesus Christ are given to us without interruption. We are NOW the sons of God, we are NOW hid with Christ in God. Christ NOW abides in us and there is therefore NOW no condemnation to them who are in Christ Jesus, who walk not after the flesh. The statement "who walk not after the flesh" does not mean IF they walk not after the flesh, but it is a strong statement meaning that because they are IN Christ Jesus THEY WILL NOT WALK AFTER THE FLESH. The Word clearly teaches, "As many as are led by the Spirit of God, they are the children of God" (Rom. 8:14). Again, "If we walk in the Spirit we will not fulfill the desires of the flesh."

In verse 23 Paul is admonishing the Colossian believers to be grounded and settled in the faith—the faith to which Jude refers, "which was once delivered to the saints." Read Ephesians 3:18; I Peter 5:10; I Corinthians 7:37; 15:58. Born again, blood-washed, saved-by-grace sons of God are founded and fixed, and "shall not be moved."

Many believers need to study and accept Ephesians 1:18: "The eyes of your understanding being enlightened; that ye may know WHAT IS THE HOPE OF HIS CALLING, and what the riches of the glory of His inheritance in the saints."

A life of true faith in the finished work of Jesus Christ, instead of faith in one's own ability or in some religion, is a life of hope—and leads to glory. True faith in the finished work of Jesus has a conservative power. Such faith keeps the justified, secures the one who is "hid with Christ in God" (Col. 3:3) and who is continuously cleansed by the precious blood of the Lamb (I John 1:7). The true Bible fact that the believer is kept by the power of God—yea, kept by God Himself—does not cause the believer to live a careless life, but rather makes him distrustful of himself and totally dependent upon God. The believer knows the truth of the warning, "Let him that thinketh he standeth take heed lest he fall" (I Cor. 10:12).

72

The true believer also knows "There hath no temptation taken you but such as is common to man: but God is faithful, who will not suffer you to be tempted above that ye are able; but will with the temptation also make a way to escape, that ye may be able to bear it" (I Cor. 10:13).

In verse 23 Paul admonishes the Colossians, ". . . And be not moved away from the hope of the Gospel." Just what is the Gospel? If we are admonished not to be moved away from the *hope* of the Gospel, what IS the Gospel in the first place? The best place to find the answer is in God's Word. In I Corinthians 15:1–8 Paul says, "Moreover, brethren, I declare unto you THE GOSPEL which I preached unto you, which also ye have received, and wherein ye stand; by which also ye are *saved*, if ye keep in memory what I preached unto you, unless ye have believed in vain. For I delivered unto you first of all that which I also received, how that CHRIST DIED FOR OUR SINS ACCORDING TO THE SCRIPTURES; AND THAT HE WAS BURIED, AND THAT HE ROSE AGAIN THE THIRD DAY ACCORDING TO THE SCRIPTURES: And that He was seen of Cephas, then of the twelve: After that, He was seen of above five hundred brethren at once; of whom the greater part remain unto this present, but some are fallen asleep. After that, he was seen of James; then of all the apostles. AND LAST OF ALL HE WAS SEEN OF ME ALSO, AS OF ONE BORN OUT OF DUE TIME."

Paul preached *the Gospel*. The Corinthians were *saved* by the Gospel, they were *standing* in the Gospel; but what did he preach? He preached what he received: *How that Christ died for our sins according to the Scriptures.* He was buried, *according to the Scriptures*; He rose again and was seen by many men, *as recorded in the Scriptures.* Paul preached a crucified, buried, risen, ascended, living Lord. *That is the Gospel*—but it must be *"according to the Scriptures."*

The errorists in the Colossian community were teaching that Jesus was not the God-man, that He did not actually die, that He was not actually raised, that He was some sort of spirit-being. Such teaching is not the Gospel. It is error, and it will damn all who believe it. Thus Paul admonished the Colossians to continue in the Gospel, to hold fast their faith in the death, burial and resurrection of Christ . . . faith in the one Mediator, the man Christ Jesus.

Paul goes further: He said, "Which ye have heard . . . ." That is, "You are informed concerning the Gospel. I have preached the Gospel to you, Timothy has preached the Gospel to you, Epaphras has preached the Gospel to you. You are not in the dark, you are children of light; so walk in the light. Continue in the light and pay no attention to these errorists."

The statement, "which was preached to every creature which is under heaven" may confuse some, but it simply means to every creature (to the whole world) known in that day. That did not take in the earth's surface as we know it today, nor the multiplied millions we have on earth today. Paul is simply saying that the Gospel had been preached throughout that area to all the people and there was no excuse for ignorance concerning it. He closes the statement by saying, "Whereof I Paul am made a minister." He was not a denomination-called preacher. He was not a self-made preacher, nor a seminary-manufactured preacher. He was a *God-called* preacher, ordained of God, sent by God—and he preached the Gospel of God without fear, favor or apology. He pleaded with the Colossians to stand by the Gospel "which ye have heard."

THE MYSTERY OF THE INDWELLING CHRIST
Verse 24: "Who now rejoice in my sufferings for

74

you, and fill up that which is behind of the afflictions of Christ in my flesh for His body's sake, which is the Church."

Verse 23 closes with the statement, "I Paul am made a minister." Verse 24 opens with "Who now rejoice in my sufferings for you." Paul rejoiced in his heart because he could suffer for the sake of the Gospel. It was because of his preaching that he was in jail at that particular time, going through torment of body and anguish of spirit and soul. In spite of his pain, he was rejoicing, happy, and his heart was filled with praise because of his sufferings for the church at Colosse, as well as for other churches where he had been used of God in Asia Minor.

The remaining part of the verse has troubled some people: "And fill up that which is behind of the afflictions of Christ in my flesh for His body's sake, which is the Church." These sufferings referred to by Paul are named by him "the afflictions of Christ." They were *Christ's sufferings* because Christ felt the blows that were put upon Paul. Paul felt pain when he was flogged, stoned and dragged outside the city for dead; he felt the dampness and cold of the prison cell; but Christ really felt the sufferings that Paul was going through because the stripes that are placed upon the believer are truly placed upon Christ. We are members of the Church (of which He is the head) and we therefore are members of His body, bone of His bone and flesh of His flesh—and *"The reproaches of them that reproached thee are fallen upon Me"* (Psalm 69:9).

Very few believers realize just how closely connected the Christian is to Christ. We are dead, and our lives are *hid with Christ in God*. We are in Him, He is in us, and thus we possess divine nature (II Peter 1:4). The Church is the body of Christ, He is the head of the

75

body—and the head suffers when the members suffer. Paul's sufferings were Christ's sufferings, for Christ is identified with all His people regardless of who or where they may be. Every born again person is a member of His body.

Read the ninth chapter of Acts. See Saul of Tarsus, with blood in his eye, murder in his heart, and a pocket filled with letters of authority as he traveled to Damascus to persecute the Christians. A light shone from heaven, and through that blinding light a voice cried out, "Saul, Saul! Why persecutest thou me?" These words clearly teach that the Redeemer was one with the flock in Damascus, soon to feel the lash of persecution as it was inflicted by Saul of Tarsus.

We read in God's precious Word that apostates who turn from their profession, who claim that they have discovered faith in Christ to be just a dream . . . a delusion . . . a myth . . . *"crucify to themselves the Son of God afresh, and put Him to an open shame"* (Heb. 6:6). Paul said, "The sufferings of Christ abound in us" (II Cor. 1:5). (He means the sufferings endured by Christ in— or *through*—believers, members of His body.)

Paul admonishes the sons of God, "Let us go forth therefore unto Him without the camp, BEARING HIS REPROACH" (Heb. 13:13). Please notice Paul did not say, "bearing reproach *on His account.*" He said, "bearing HIS reproach"—the reproach which is His . . . the reproach He still bears in us through our living connection with Him (II Cor. 2:10).

Concerning Moses, Paul says, "By faith Moses, when he was come to years, refused to be called the son of Pharaoh's daughter; *choosing rather to suffer affliction with the people of God, . . . esteeming the reproach of Christ* greater riches than the treasures in

76

Egypt: for he had respect unto the recompence of the reward" (Heb. 11:24–26). No man ever had a chance to be exalted to a higher position or greater glory than did Moses; but he counted *the reproach of Christ* greater by far than all the riches of Egypt. God help me to have a bit of the spirit of Moses as I travel this journey!

In the Gospels on many occasions Jesus declared the oneness between Himself and His people. He said, "I and my Father are one"—*and they took up stones to stone Him*! He prayed in John 17 that believers on earth would be one, even as He and the Father are one. He declares His oneness with His people today in that He lives within them, endures the pangs of hunger and thirst, feels pain, heat, cold. In them He is tired and weary, fed and refreshed. With His people He endures imprisonment, He knows every heartbeat and every heartache. He knows and is concerned about every need; and He joys exceedingly in withholding no good thing from them who walk uprightly.

It is true that He suffered *once—for all, forever—* never to suffer again insofar as His person is concerned; but His sufferings in His people will continue until the consummation of all things. Then, thank God, He Himself will wipe all tears from their eyes. There will be no more crying, no more pain. Former things will be past forever!

Verse 25: "Whereof I am made a minister, according to the dispensation of God which is given to me for you, to fulfill the Word of God." The original language here reads, "Of which church I was made a minister." Paul was not a minister just to the Colossians, but to *the Church*, the body of Christ. Wherever sinners needed to hear the Gospel of salvation, wherever babes in Christ needed the milk of the Word or growing believers needed *meat*, Paul was made a minister! He was certainly a hero of the faith. The Church had never known such a minister—a man with such enthusiasm and perseverance, such sufferings and opposition—yet such success—as he had.

I doubt not that Paul was the instrument used of God to convert more souls than any other man of his day. He did not even rest when they chained him in prison! He continued to preach and teach, writing to the churches and witnessing for the Saviour who had so gloriously changed his whole life and being. Paul's ministry is singular and superlative: Measure the miles he traveled, count the sermons he preached, add up the stripes he received and the stonings he endured—all for the sake of the Gospel. This man was in hunger and thirst, in cold and nakedness (II Cor. 11:23–27).

Count the churches he founded and to which he ministered, visiting them in person and writing epistles to them when he could not visit them. Count the letters he wrote—and then remove the shoes from your feet when you read the account of how he died! And yet—he said to Timothy, in essence, "If I had another life to live, I would live it *for the Gospel.* I have fought a good fight, I have finished my course. I have kept the faith. Henceforth there is laid up for me a crown of life. For to me to live is Christ—TO DIE IS GAIN!"

At the end of a stormy—yet joyous and exceedingly successful ministry, just before his head rolled under the headsman's axe, Paul looked at death. He did not preach a short sermon on "An Axe, a Coffin, and a Grave." Instead, he left a glowing testimony: *"This is my pay day!* To me, *to die is gain!"* I repeat: The Church has never known such another minister as Paul . . . such a stalwart hero of the faith.

Paul's ministry was "according to the dispensation of God." He looked upon his ministry and his office in the work of the Lord as a distinctive calling to a Gentile group—and he gloried in it. He refused to be confined within a narrow circuit; he refused to bow to Judaism: *his field was the world.* I wonder how Paul would get along today with some of the modern spiritual leaders who do not want anyone to infringe upon their parish? If an evangelist moves into a community, rents an auditorium for services or sets up a gospel tent for revival, he is often reminded, "We have our churches, we have our preachers. This is our parish, and we will take care of the spiritual needs here."

The world was Paul's parish—and the Scriptural command is, "Go ye *into all the world,* and preach the Gospel to every creature." No minister has any right to stake off a community and say, "This is MY parish!" Paul was called to "fulfill the Word of God." He was a special vessel, a special minister; he did not confer with the spiritual fathers at Jerusalem when he set out on his journey in the ministry. He did more than preach— *he fulfilled the Gospel* . . . he carried out the program of Almighty God. He held up to the world the healing balm of Gilead. He proclaimed the Gospel without distinction of race or creed. This Apostle to the Gentiles carried the Gospel to all who would listen, both in and beyond the boundaries of Judaea. He lifted the blood-stained banner above the walls of the Jewish synagogue, yet held it high to *all nations* and *all people.* Paul gave his life preaching the Gospel everywhere, to all classes, without distinction. He labored "to fulfill the Word of God." Read Luke 7:1; 9:31; Acts 13:25; 14:26.

Verse 26: "Even the mystery which hath been hid from ages and from generations, but now is made manifest to his saints."

God called and ordained Paul, and gave to him by revelation the unveiling of the mystery that had been

79

hidden in the ages since the beginning . . . which mystery was the great doctrine that salvation was to be proclaimed to all mankind, regardless of color or class, Jew or Gentile. Paul was to make this mystery fully known. This great hidden truth had been concealed unto Paul's day, "but now is made manifest to His saints."

The mystery is no longer a mystery! The truth has been communicated to the apostles—men ordained of God and commissioned by God—who were appointed to proclaim and make known the truth that the Gentiles could and would be fellow heirs with all saints. Paul knew that he was called to make this truth known——that is, as far as it is possible for mankind to understand the the glorious truth of "Christ in you, the hope of glory."

His letter to the church at Ephesus gives a little more light on the mystery: "For this cause I Paul, the prisoner of Jesus Christ for you Gentiles, if ye have heard of the dispensation of the grace of God which is given me to you-ward: How that by revelation He made known unto me the mystery; (as I wrote afore in few words, whereby, when ye read, ye may understand my knowledge in the mystery of Christ) which in other ages was not made known unto the sons of men, as it is now revealed unto His holy apostles and prophets by the Spirit; THAT THE GENTILES SHOULD BE FELLOWHEIRS, AND OF THE SAME BODY, AND PARTAKERS OF HIS PROMISE IN CHRIST BY THE GOSPEL: Whereof I was made a minister, according to the gift of the grace of God given unto me by the effectual working of His power. Unto me, who am less than the least of all saints, is this grace given, that I should preach among the Gentiles the unsearchable riches of Christ; and to make all men see what is the fellowship of the mystery, which from the beginning of the world hath been hid in God, who created all things by Jesus Christ: to the intent that now unto the principalities and powers in heavenly places might be known by the church the manifold wisdom of God, according to the eternal purpose which He purposed in Christ Jesus our Lord: In whom we have boldness and access with confidence by the faith of Him" (Eph. 3:1–12).

In these verses, Paul clearly declares that God called him for a specific purpose, to make known the dispensation of the grace of God, to reveal through him the mystery that the Gentiles could be saved and become sons of God—fellow heirs with the Jews and with *"who- soever."* Paul's ministry was to make all men see what is the fellowship of the mystery, and to declare the eternal purpose which God purposed in Christ Jesus our Lord.

The mystery "hid in God" referred to here was God's divine program and purpose to unite Jew and Gentile in one body ("the Church, which is Christ's body")—certainly a new thing not known before. God revealed to Paul how the body would be formed by the baptism of the Holy Ghost. In I Corinthians 12:12–13 we are told that "as the body is one, and hath many members, and all the members of that one body, being many, are one body: so also is Christ, for by one Spirit are we all baptized into one body, whether we be Jews or Gentiles, whether we be bond or free; and have been all made to drink into one Spirit."

Whether you be Jew or Gentile, black or white, learned or unlearned, rich or poor—if you have exercised faith in the Lord Jesus and you are trusting in His shed blood, having received Him by faith, *you have been baptized by the Holy Ghost into the body of Christ.* When an unbeliever believes unto salvation and is united to the body of Christ by the baptism of the Holy Spirit, the distinction of race and color disappears (Eph. 2:14,15; Col. 3:10,11). To the Apostle Paul, God revealed this great mystery.

The mystery was foretold by the Lord Jesus, but it was not time for the explanation. Jesus asked His disciples, ". . . Whom say ye that I am? And Simon Peter answered and said, *Thou art the Christ, the Son of the living God! . . .* Jesus answered and said unto him, Blessed art thou, Simon Bar-jona: for *flesh and blood hath not revealed it unto thee*, but my Father which is in heaven. And I say unto thee, That thou art Peter, and *upon this rock I will build my church; and the gates of hell shall not prevail against it*" (Matt. 16:15–18). Jesus did not explain the mystery of His declaration. The *rock* was the testimony Peter had just given concerning Christ: *Christ is the Rock!* Jesus made known the *coming* of the Church, but to Paul was committed the revelation of the mystery. It is in the writings of Paul alone that we find the *doctrine* for the New Testament Church, the *position* of the Church, the *walk of the believer*, and the *destiny of the entire body when it is complete.*

Verse 27: "To whom God would make known what is the riches of the glory of this mystery among the Gentiles; which is Christ in you, the hope of glory."

"*To whom God would make known . . . .*" In other words, Paul said, "You are the persons to whom God wished to make known the riches of the glory of the mystery among the Gentiles." It was God's good pleasure to make known the glorious redemption in Christ's blood. It was not a divine imperative; it was a divine *pleasure* to reveal to the Colossians that the Gentiles had been accepted by God through the death of the Lord Jesus. The saints did not discover the mystery for themselves through their own knowledge and wisdom. Christianity did not spring up because of their wisdom, understanding or good works: *Christianity was made known by Almighty God.* The mystery was unfolded to Paul by

82

revelation. He did not enter the seminary and discover it in books of Theology, nor did he dig it out by himself. God *revealed* it to him; God unfolded before Paul what had been hidden from all men, from Adam up to the time of the Apostle Paul.

"*Christ in you . . . .*" The mystery revealed is "*Christ in you*, the hope of glory." Do not confuse the statement "this mystery among the Gentiles" with the revelation of the mystery, "Christ IN you." Christ was not just *among* the Gentiles, but Christ literally took up His abode IN the Gentiles who believed on Him in saving faith. It was not just *to know Christ*, but to *possess Christ* in the heart by faith.

"*The hope of glory.*" The final glory of believers is yet to come, but it is as sure to come as God is God. Believers are strangers and pilgrims on earth. What true believers earnestly pray for and long for, and what they labor to possess, shall be revealed in glory far beyond our anticipation. In the final glory, because of the grace of the Lord Jesus Christ, we will be delivered from all evil. We will possess all good . . . all the good that God can provide. What we have partially enjoyed here, we will fully enjoy and possess in heaven—yea, "All things!" What has seemed glory in this life will be feeble as compared to "*far more exceeding and eternal weight of glory*" (II Cor. 4:17b).

Man, in his natural body, cannot see God . . . frail humanity would be consumed by His brightness and glory; but we will receive a body so prepared that we can look with unmingled rapture upon His indescribable majesty and glory. We will receive a body prepared by Him (I John 3:1–3) in order that we may *live* with Him and *walk* with Him. There are no adjectives or words to describe the glorified body of Jesus, and we will have a body just like His glorious body. We will be filled with light from the face of God and we will walk in the light from His face.

All believers will enjoy uninterrupted fellowship with Him, we will all live next door to Him and will be in His presence forever. All things will have been made new, nothing that *has been* will remain. Therefore nothing can happen to disrupt this perfect communion and perfect fellowship—this *"exceeding and eternal weight of glory."* The devil, the beast, the false prophet and all the demons will be in the lake of fire. No evil will ever invade "all things made new." Every person to enter that celestial glory will be just as perfect as Jesus is perfect—in soul, in body, in spirit, in every way. There will be no more pain, no more sorrow, no more tears, "no graves on the hillsides of glory, no funeral trains in the sky," no crepe on the doorknob and no mourning. It will be a day when death is swallowed up of life—but never forget that CHRIST IS THE HOPE OF THIS GLORY! Adam forfeited the glory of the Paradise of Eden; but thank God, Jesus has bought back, through His blood, everything Adam lost; and when we receive the Lord Jesus as our Saviour, the hope of glory is ours.

All have sinned and come short of the glory of God. Even David, a man after God's own heart, declared, "I was born in sin and shapen in iniquity." Isaiah declared, "All we like sheep have gone astray." By nature, all men are doomed to die—but faith in Christ brings *new* nature, *new* life. "Christ in you" is *divine nature* in you. "Christ in you" is *eternal life in you,* because *Christ cannot die.*

The believer's justification is in Christ (Rom. 5:1,2). Since Christ died once, to die no more, who can cancel our justification? Who shall condemn the true believer? Sin may lift its ugly head to condemn us, *but Christ made an end of sin*; He suffered for sin; He bore our sins in

His own body on the cross: *"Who His own self bare our sins in His own body on the tree, that we, being dead to sins, should live unto righteousness: by whose stripes ye were healed"* (I Peter 2:24). Sin has been dealt with — once, for all, forever.

Should Satan attempt to condemn us, we must remember that Jesus personally met Satan and defeated him (Matt. 4:1 ff). Satan hurled at Jesus everything hell had; but when the battle was over, the devil was defeated and angels ministered to Jesus, strengthening Him. Jesus conquered the flesh, the devil, death, hell and the grave. With "Christ in you" Satan's mouth has been stopped insofar as condemning the believer is concerned.

Shall our conscience condemn us? If Christ is within, the conscience has been purged from dead works. If we are true believers, our heart condemns us not.

Can death terrify the believer? Jesus personally declared war on death, conquered death, and from death took the keys (Rev. 1:18).

"Who shall lay anything to the charge of God's elect?" Who shall condemn us? In Christ we are more than conquerors, and it can be said of every true Christian, "Christ is within — and we are hid with Christ in God" (Col. 1:27; 3:3). We are more than conquerors because "greater is He that is within you than he that is in the world" (I John 4:4). To every believer God says in His Word, "Now the God of hope fill you with all joy and peace in believing, that ye may abound in hope, through the power of the Holy Ghost" (Rom. 15:13). Such words inspire the Christian. When we realize that our hope is Christ, and Christ is in us, it gives us faith that is unshakeable.

As believers, we look *behind* us and see Christ on the cross *for us.* Daily we look *about* us and see His promises and pledges to us, sealed in His blood; and not one promise spoken can ever be broken, because *God cannot lie* (Heb. 6:18; Titus 1:2). When we look ahead and upward, we are strengthened with the assurance that this may be the day when the trumpet will sound, when we will be changed "in a moment, in the twinkling of an eye."

"If God be for us, who can be against us?" I am glad it was Paul who wrote those words, because I think he suffered as no other but Jesus ever suffered. He knew Christ, he knew Christ was all-sufficient, regardless of the need. What a glorious change to the Gentile world! Up to that point, Gentiles had been aliens, strangers to the commonwealth of Israel, "dogs," hopeless and without God; but now through the blood of Jesus (the grace of our God in Christ), Gentiles can become sons—heirs of God and joint heirs with Christ.

Verse 28: "Whom we preach, warning every man, and teaching every man in all wisdom; that we may present every man perfect in Christ Jesus."

Verse 27 closes with the clear, understandable statement, *"Christ* in you, the hope of glory." Verse 28 opens with *"whom we preach,"* referring to Christ. Paul had a singular message: *Christ.* He said, "I count all things but loss for the excellency of the knowledge of Christ Jesus my Lord" (Phil. 3:8). Everywhere he preached, his theme was *"Jesus Christ—*crucified, buried, risen and coming again" (Acts 17:3; Phil. 1:17). To Paul, Christ was glorious in His person and perfect in His ministry: *He satisifed Almighty God.* To Paul, Christ was God incarnate—the bleeding Peacemaker, Governor of the universe, because it pleased the Father that in His Christ, the Son of His love, all fullness dwelt. To Paul, it was "Christ—*whom we preach."* Paul did not preach the *doctrine* of Christ—he preached CHRIST.

Paul did not attempt to be spectacular. He did not desire to be advertised as "the world's greatest Bible teacher," nor did he crave to be known as the world's number one evangelist. Christ Jesus, the one and undivided all-sufficient Saviour was the singular subject of his preaching. Paul did not preach high-sounding messages, but his preaching was definite and precise, clearly set forth in words easily understood. He did not speculate in the things unknown to man, he did not announce subjects concerning mysteries that are secrets known only to Jehovah God. He did not deal in meats and drinks, days and garments. He preached Christ—the Man, the Person, the Mediator, in whom we are complete. He did not cater to crowds who desired to be gratified by prying into the celestial arena of spirits and angels. He did not suggest that angels should be worshipped or prayed to. He never substituted anything for Jesus Christ. His message was faith, hope, love—all wrapped up in Jesus, the greatest of these being love, because God is love and Christ is God. His one theme was Christ, in whom we have pardon by His blood, by whose Spirit we possess purity, righteousness and, eventually, *perfection* without spot or wrinkle when we shall stand in His presence.

". . . *Warning every man.*" Paul's message was to all men, regardless of race, creed or color. He warned the sinner to repent, believe, trust, 'ere he stand before God alone—condemned, helpless, hopeless and hell-bound. He warned the Christian to present his body a living sacrifice, his members as instruments of righteousness, and whether eating, drinking, or whatsoever the believer should do, all should be done to the glory of God.

Paul emphasizes "every man": "teaching *every man* in all wisdom." To the Corinthians Paul said, "Christ is made unto us wisdom, righteousness, sanctification and redemption, that no flesh should glory in His presence." Christ is perfect wisdom. Paul preached Christ—the Person. He preached the Gospel in wisdom for the specific purpose of guiding sinners to Christ and away from the lies of the errorist. He urged the unbeliever to accept free and full salvation . . . *by grace, through faith.* He begged the Christian to present his all to God, and to look to God for comfort, strength and abundant fruit-bearing. He preached the Gospel in all wisdom.

I doubt that Paul would be invited to speak in some of our churches today. I refer to the groups who feel that they are the elect, select, predestined and chosen, and that all others are left out. The Apostle Paul dwelt on individuals. He preached the individualizing character of the pure Gospel of grace. He uses the words *"every man"* three times in verse 28: *"warning* every man . . . *teaching* every man . . . that we may *present* every man." Paul was trying to drive home to the Colossians the glorious truth that Christ died for every man, loves every man, and longs to save every man.

Paul felt a tremendous debt to every man. In Romans 1:14—16 he declares, "I am debtor both to the Greeks, and to the Barbarians; both to the wise, and to the unwise. So, as much as in me is, I am ready to preach the Gospel to you that are at Rome also. For I am not ashamed of the Gospel of Christ: for it is the power of God unto salvation to every one that believeth; to the Jew first, and also to the Greek." Paul had a deep, undying interest in every man, whatever his character or creed. Every man on earth—regardless of his race or lineage, his heritage or his station in life—shared in the heartfelt sympathy, the burning desire of Paul to see ALL men saved and presented to Christ. Every man had a place in Paul's prayers. He did not pray limited prayers for a limited group. He prayed for all.

The motive for Paul's preaching and for his prayers

is stated in the last of verse 28: ". . . that we may present every man perfect in Christ Jesus." Certainly not every man was perfected whom he had endeavored to instruct; but that did not keep him from having a *deep desire* to see every man saved. He refused to be content with anything less.

Concerning his own people, Paul said in Romans 9:1–3, "I say the truth in Christ, I lie not, my conscience also bearing me witness in the Holy Ghost, that I have great heaviness and continual sorrow in my heart. For I could wish that myself were accursed from Christ for my brethren, my kinsmen according to the flesh." In essence he was saying, "I would be willing to be cut off from Christ and burn in hell if that would save my people." Study those verses—and feel the heartbeat of this great Apostle.

Verse 29: "Whereunto I also labour, striving according to His working, which worketh in me mightily."

The ministry was not a sideline with Paul; it was not something he did lightly, a frivolous work to pass away the time. The ministry made a demand upon every faculty of the Apostle and upon every moment of his time. To Timothy, his son in the Gospel, he said, "For therefore we both labour and suffer reproach, because we trust in the living God, who is the Saviour of all men, specially of those that believe" (I Tim. 4:10).

Paul had many enemies with which to contend (Phil. 1:29,30; I Tim. 6:5; II Thess. 3:2). These verses go much deeper than physical enemies who would hinder Paul's ministry. I believe they refer to an agony of spiritual earnestness in the heart of the Apostle. I believe he spent hours in agonizing prayer—prayer that produced many tears.

The ministry is not only a divine duty, but also a

God-given privilege. A minister should be happy to exhaust his strength in performing the duties of his ministry. It is certainly an honor to wear out one's life in the true ministry of the Gospel. Paul was just such a preacher. The heart that beat within his bosom was not a sluggish heart; his zeal was not lukewarm—but torrid. There was a keenness in his emotions and anxieties that made him singular among ministers . . . every thought, every action, every effort was for Christ's sake. Said he, *"I count all things loss, that I might win Christ."* He was fervent in spirit, untiring in labor, and he gave credit where credit was due.

In the last part of the verse, Paul confesses that his striving for the souls of men is according to *"His working, which worketh in me mightily."* ("His" refers to none other than Christ Jesus.) Paul was a dedicated servant—soul, spirit and body. He labored not only under divine instruction and divine energy, but he labored just as far as divine energy enabled him to labor. Hear him as he says, *"By the grace of God I am what I am: and His grace which was bestowed upon me was not in vain, but I labored more abundantly than they all: yet not I, BUT THE GRACE OF GOD WHICH WAS WITH ME"* (I Cor. 15:10).

Paul received his message by *divine revelation*. He delivered that message by *divine power*. He said, "I can do all things through Christ which strengtheneth me" (Phil. 4:13). His singular motive was to present every man perfect in Christ, through the preaching of Christ, and he knew that this could be accomplished only through the power of Christ. He knew human power and influence could not change the hearts of men.

A minister may learn the methods and the genius of building a great organization and drawing great crowds; but without grace, holiness and spiritual support, any ministry is vain. "OUR SUFFICIENCY IS OF GOD" (II Cor. 3:5,6).

COLOSSIANS –– CHAPTER TWO

1. For I would that ye knew what great conflict I have for you, and for them at Laodicea, and for as many as have not seen my face in the flesh;

2. That their hearts might be comforted, being knit together in love, and unto all riches of the full assurance of understanding, to the acknowledgement of the mystery of God, and of the Father, and of Christ;

3. In whom are hid all the treasures of wisdom and knowledge.

4. And this I say, lest any man should beguile you with enticing words.

5. For though I be absent in the flesh, yet am I with you in the spirit, joying and beholding your order, and the stedfastness of your faith in Christ.

6. As ye have therefore received Christ Jesus the Lord, so walk ye in him:

7. Rooted and built up in him, and stablished in the faith, as ye have been taught, abounding therein with thanksgiving.

8. Beware lest any man spoil you through philosophy and vain deceit, after the tradition of men, after the rudiments of the world, and not after Christ.

9. For in him dwelleth all the fulness of the Godhead bodily.

10. And ye are complete in him, which is the head of all principality and power:

11. In whom also ye are circumcised with the circumcision made without hands, in putting off the body of the sins of the flesh by the circumcision of Christ:

12. Buried with him in baptism, wherein also ye are risen with him through the faith of the operation of God, who hath raised him from the dead.

13. And you, being dead in your sins and the uncircumcision of your flesh, hath he quickened together with him, having forgiven you all trespasses;

14. Blotting out the handwriting of ordinances that was against us, which was contrary to us, and took it out of the way, nailing it to his cross;

15. And having spoiled principalities and powers, he made a shew of them openly, triumphing over them in it.

16. Let no man therefore judge you in meat, or in drink, or in respect of an holyday, or of the new moon, or of the sabbath days:

17. Which are a shadow of things to come; but the body is of Christ.

18. Let no man beguile you of your reward in a voluntary humility and worshipping of angels, intruding into those things which he hath not seen, vainly puffed up by his fleshly mind,

19. And not holding the Head, from which all the body by joints and bands having nourishment ministered, and knit together, increaseth with the increase of God.

20. Wherefore if ye be dead with Christ from the rudiments of the world, why, as though living in the world, are ye subject to ordinances,

21. (Touch not; taste not; handle not;

22. Which all are to perish with the using;) after the commandments and doctrines of men?

23. Which things have indeed a shew of wisdom in will worship, and humility, and neglecting of the body; not in any honour to the satisfying of the flesh.

THE GODHEAD INCARNATE IN CHRIST

The Believer is Complete in Christ

The closing verses of chapter 1 reveal Paul's sufferings for the Church. A deep, burning desire to make known free salvation to all men filled the heart and dominated the spirit of the great Apostle, making him the great minister that he was and eventually leading him to a martyr's death. The value of souls and the glory of Christ dwelt in his heart; his every thought and desire was to reach these jewels for Christ to the glory of God.

It was Paul's heart-desire that the Gospel should be preserved in all its purity and simplicity of free grace minus works and without the mixture of Judaism or false philosophy. He knew the teaching of the errorists in Colosse would introduce erroneous doctrine that would rob precious souls of salvation; he knew sinners would be damned because of the error of these teachers. He knew that the Word of God brings saving faith (Rom. 10:17), and he knew a religion without blood and the cross would damn souls instead of saving them.

93

Paul displayed no favoritism; he preached alike to one and all. He delivered the same message in all communities where he preached. He was not jealous of his fellow ministers; he loved and prayed for the churches which he had not visited in person, those "who had not seen his face." Therefore, he opens chapter two with this declaration:

Verse 1: "For I would that ye knew what great conflict I have for you, and for them at Laodicea, and for as many as have not seen my face in the flesh."

In reality, there should not be a chapter division here, because this verse is a continuation of the thought in verses 28 and 29 of the preceding chapter. Paul was undergoing painful anxiety concerning the believers at Colosse and some of the other churches; his soul was in distress for them. He knew the errorists would do all in their ungodly power to cause the Colossians to accept their false doctrine, and he also knew that if such false doctrine gained a foothold, there was a possibility of the great church at Colosse falling into apostasy and becoming fruitless instead of the great fruitbearing church that it was.

Paul knew what was at stake. It was no easy burden for him, and he had labored untiringly, he had given his best, had suffered for the Gospel of grace. He had lifted up the God-Man, and now the errorists were attempting to tear down what he had so untiringly built up through the preaching of the Gospel. Paul loved these believers with a deeper love than that which you and I have for our children, our own flesh and blood. It was not the dampness of the Roman prison that broke his heart, nor yet the darkness of the dungeon and lack of food to strengthen his physical body: His heart was crushed because of his children in the Gospel—the churches he had established in that part of God's great vineyard. He cried out, "I wish you knew what great conflict I have for you!"

Paul seems to suggest that if the believers knew how heavy was his heart because of the possibility that some of the babes in Christ might fall into apostasy under the teaching of errorists, they would pay no attention to the false teachers. Not only is Paul concerned about the believers in the Colossian church, but also the believers at Laodicea and throughout that part of Asia Minor—even those churches where he had not had the privilege of visiting.

Verse 2: "That their hearts might be comforted, being knit together in love, and unto all riches of the full assurance of understanding, to the acknowledgement of the mystery of God, and of the Father, and of Christ."

Hope is found only in truth. Truth brings comfort and assurance, while error brings discomfort and creates distrust. In the community of the Colossians there was a conflict between error and truth. Paul knew that such conflict could only lead to mental turmoil and distrust, thereby producing discomfort in the hearts of some of the Colossians—especially those who were still babes in Christ.

The church situation in Paul's day was different from that of today. That was the transition period and Christianity was a new religion, while Judaism was an accepted religion; some of the error being taught in the early church was a mixture of Judaism and other "isms." Paul knew this would have its effect on the believers and he did not want them to sacrifice one moment of their peace, comfort and rejoicing in the new religion of Christianity they had so recently embraced. He wanted them to be united in love, *"knit together in love."*

During the years of my ministry I have seen families

divided because of religion; I have seen churches split, families separated, parents and children refusing to speak to one another. I have known neighbors who were friends for years—yet who because of a church split have lost fellowship and refused to speak one to the other. Such a spirit is exceedingly ugly in the sight of God, and such a spirit in a community will break the heart of any true pastor. Thus Paul's prayer and deep desire for the Colossian believers was that they "being compacted together," would be united in love to the extent that there would be no schism in the local assembly.

Error begets suspicion between brethren and friends. Where error enters, there will be a tendency to question others, a tendency to wonder to what degree others have accepted the error, thus bringing about much argument and creating dissension. What people say will be weighed more carefully and many times offence is taken where no offence is intended. Paul was very anxious that the Colossian church suffer no such tragedy. He wanted them to be bound together in mutual, affectionate *oneness*; he wanted them to prove their Christianity by loving one another—for if we believers love not our brother whom we have seen, how can we love God whom we have not seen?

". . . And unto all riches of the full assurance of understanding . . . ." In order to love persons or earthly things with pure love, it is necessary to know them fully; but in the spiritual aspect *it is necessary to love the spiritual* in order to *know* it (I Cor. 2:14). We must love the things of God as we search His Word to know spiritual things more perfectly. Paul wanted the Colossians to enjoy "the full assurance of understanding." He wanted them to fully comprehend the truth and to be sure it was *truth* they were accepting TO understand. He wanted them to know the truth, accept the truth, be established

96

in the truth, and not be driven about with every wind of doctrine. If a professing Christian believes one thing today and something else tomorrow; if he holds to one doctrine today but lets go of it and accepts another tomorrow; if the professing Christian is continually accepting new impressions and announcing new convictions, then that person belongs to the assembly referred to as "ever learning, but never able to come to the knowledge of the truth." Such religion is of the devil and such a way leads to destruction. "There is a way that seemeth right unto a man, but the end thereof are the ways of death" (Prov. 16:25).

Lack of true Bible knowledge is the reason there is so much confusion today among professing Christians. A believer whose mind is fixed concerning spiritual things as taught in the Word of God will not be easily led astray by false teachers. If Christians are rooted and grounded in the faith once and for all delivered unto the saints, they will not be driven about with every wind of doctrine. The person who is easily influenced by those who teach error is a person who is spiritually a "fence straddler" or a "middle-of-the-roader" who with a little push may fall either way.

Thank God for the assurance of I Peter 2:6: "Behold, I lay in Sion a chief corner stone, elect, precious: and he that believeth on Him shall not be confounded (confused)." I praise God for that verse. When we know the truth, the truth makes us free. When we believe on Jesus and trust Him fully, the Holy Ghost leads us into truth and guards us against error (I John 2:27).

Verse 2 closes with the statement, ". . . to the acknowledgement of the mystery of God, and of the Father, and of Christ." The mystery has already been explained in Colossians 1:27: *"Christ in you, the hope of glory."* Paul wanted the Colossians to boldly and publicly testify that they were believers in God's Christ—believing that Christ was God and God was Christ, believing fully in the incarnation, believing without reservation that *Christ in the heart is the only hope of reaching heaven.* He wanted the Colossian believers to be assured in their hearts of this fundamental truth; he wanted them to fully understand (as far as it is possible for man to understand) the mystery of the incarnation. He wanted them to be sure they fully understood that God the Father, God the Son and God the Holy Ghost *all are responsible* for our redemption: God the Father loved us; God the Son died for us; God the Holy Spirit draws us, "borns" us, baptizes us into the body of Christ, and then indwells and seals us until the day of redemption.

Verse 3: *"In whom* are hid all the treasures of wisdom and knowledge." In connection with verse 3 we should study Ephesians 1:9—10: "Having made known unto us the mystery of His will, according to His good pleasure which He hath purposed in Himself: That in the dispensation of the fulness of times He might gather together in one all things in Christ, both which are in heaven, and which are on earth; even in Him." (Also study Ephesians 3:9: "And to make all men see what is the fellowship of the mystery, which from the beginning of the world hath been hid in God, who created all things by Jesus Christ.")

The literal Greek reading in Colossians 2:3 gives us the word "wherein" instead of "in whom." That is, *"Wherein"* is the mystery (that Jews and Gentiles would be one in Christ through His substitutionary death).

What Paul is saying to believers is this: "You need not go in search of higher truth and loftier science, for *in Christ* is found all wisdom, all knowledge, and *we are complete in Him.* Christ is made unto us wisdom, righteousness, sanctification and redemption. In Christ we find "all the treasures of wisdom and knowledge." The heart desire of Paul is that the believers at Colosse will learn through searching the Scriptures, and that, believing the epistle he is directing to them, they will learn the value of the mystery, cling to it, enthrone it in their hearts, study it with diligence, and search the Scriptures instead of searching the things preached by the errorists.

The deep meaning of what Paul says in verse 3 is that in this mystery, hidden through the ages until it was revealed to him, is stored up all the treasures of wisdom and knowledge—not *partial* wisdom, not a *few fragments* of knowledge—but ALL knowledge, ALL wisdom. Paul is driving home to the hearts of the believers at Colosse the solemn fact that all they need (all any poor depraved sinner needs) is to be found in the Lord Jesus Christ. The *fulness of all things* dwells in Him—not in the philosophy and teaching of the errorists. Paul desires for his spiritual children that they will yearn for the knowledge that only the Lord Jesus supplies. Only in Him is found spiritual satisfaction and peace of heart and mind. Spiritualistic philosophy can never supply what childlike faith in the Son of God supplies to the hungry heart. Paul preached that in Jesus is to be found all the fulness of the Godhead. The *wisdom* of God, the *fulness* of God, the *glory* of God, the *holiness* of God, the *salvation* of God are revealed in the Gospel and only in the Gospel.

We learn these things by searching with a diligent heart and a Spirit-led mind. Paul said to Timothy, his son in the ministry, "Study to shew thyself approved unto God, a workman that needeth not to be ashamed, rightly dividing the word of truth" (II Tim. 2:15). The height of divine love is to be found in the revealed mystery that had been hidden in God through the ages. We learn as we study the Word of God and as the Spirit reveals to us the deep things of God, that through the shed blood of Jesus atonement has been provided for unworthy, hell-deserving sinners—atonement that no human wisdom, knowledge or ability could ever have provided. Atonement is a human impossibility; it had to come from God. In the blood of Jesus, God can be just—and yet justify the ungodly. The atonement pardons the guilty sinner without affecting the holy Law of God and its authority.

The errorists in Colosse could not accept the fact that God had robed Himself in flesh, that He had come down to earth to mix and mingle with men who were born in sin and shapen in iniquity; and in a body of flesh *God in Christ* did what the Law could not do because of the weakness of the flesh. God's Law is holy, it is not weak; but through the weakness of the *flesh* the Law could not justify the ungodly.

God in the person of Jesus came into the world, was tempted in all points as we are, yet was without sin. God in Christ carried our sins to the cross and there died the death of a criminal, that criminals might be set free! God robed Himself in humanity in order that He might redeem guilty men—men who by nature were the children of wrath, men who could not redeem themselves because of their fallen nature. But the God-Man was God AND man; the offended (God) was wrapped up in flesh such as the offender (man) possessed, and in the same body God (the offended and the offender combined) tabernacled on this earth—God in Christ, reconciling the world unto Himself (II Cor. 5:19). Such knowledge cannot be accepted nor appreciated by the natural man because the natural man receiveth not the things of God (I Cor. 2:14). The natural man walks by sight, by understanding, by wisdom—but "the just shall live by *faith*" (Rom. 1:17b). The teachers of error in Colosse refused to accept the teaching that Jesus was God in flesh.

Regardless of how many universities one may have attended, regardless of the degrees he may have earned, no man has true knowledge until he fears God (Prov. 1:7) and accepts the Word of God as the final authority on all things, whether spiritual or secular. The Word of God plainly declares that Christ was God in flesh—and that settles it. The Word of God clearly declares that without the shedding of blood is no remission—and that settles it. Jesus said, "No man can come to my Father except by me," and that is final, regardless of what men teach or preach.

Thousands of men have spent their lives in search of how this earth *became* earth; they have given their lives in laboratories and places of learning, searching for an answer to how the planets and solar systems were formed, where man came from, how he evolved to his present position; but the answers are found only in the Word of God. If those men would accept the Word of God they would have the answers to the mystery of man's origin, the mystery of nature, and the mystery of destiny. ALL mystery clears up in Christ, because in Him is found all fulness; in Him are hidden all the treasures of wisdom and knowledge.

"Where is the wise? Where is the scribe? Where is the disputer of the world? Hath God not made foolish the wisdom of this world?" (I Cor. 1:20). Let them all come, see, learn and understand: In the divine plan of redemption—planned, programmed, blueprinted and provided by God alone—all things are made clear. "WHO CAN, BY SEARCHING, FIND OUT GOD; WHO CAN FIND OUT THE ALMIGHTY UNTO PERFECTION?"

The God who created man from the dust of the earth and breathed into his nostrils the breath of life; the God

101

who so loved the world that He gave His only begotten Son that hell-deserving sinners might become sons of God, heirs of God and joint heirs with Christ; the God who provides *all things in Christ* is not found in a test tube in a laboratory nor on a slide under a microscope. He is not discovered by a speeding satellite in outer space. *He is found by the person who hears His Word, who believes with the faith of a child, who receives without question the finished work of the Lamb of God on Calvary.* Jesus declares it in these words: "Verily, verily, I say unto you, He that heareth my word, and believeth on Him that sent me, hath everlasting life, and shall not come into condemnation; but is passed from death unto life" (John 5:24).

These words were dictated to John the Beloved by Jesus, the only begotten Son. Later, under inspiration, John wrote: "He that believeth on the Son of God hath the witness in himself: he that believeth not God hath made Him a liar; because he believeth not the record that God gave of His Son: And this is the record, that God hath given to us eternal life, and this life is in His Son. He that hath the Son hath life; and he that hath not the Son of God hath not life. These things have I written unto you that believe on the name of the Son of God; that ye may know that ye have eternal life, and that ye may believe on the name of the Son of God" (I John 5:10–13).

The "little child" finds God in the Word. Hear the Word, believe the Word. The Word is the record God has given to man—the record concerning His Son. Hear the Word, for hearing brings faith. Faith, placed in the Christ of whom the Word is the record, brings salvation. We are saved by God's grace through faith; God provides the grace in the finished work of Christ, and God provides the faith to accept His grace when we hear the Word. Never forget that *what God demands, God provides.* In

Christ all fulness dwells—and "ye are complete in Him."

Tens of thousands stumble into hell over the simplicity of salvation; they try to find salvation through wisdom. The preaching of the cross is foolishness to them—they cannot accept such a simple message, they cannot receive such a free, "no strings attached" salvation. They want to reason out something, *give* something, *do* something or *be* something; but Jesus said, "Come unto me . . . I will give you rest." The Holy Spirit cries out through the pen of the Beloved Apostle, "As many as received Him . . . ." Jesus said to His own people, "And you will not come to me that you might have life!" There are many today who search the Scriptures, who study and attempt to bring God to a laboratory or classroom and dissect Him with the scalpel of human thinking. Man today is attempting to bring God down to his own level—but God will never permit that. We must *accept Him by faith and we must live by faith*; God has no other plan. It pleased God that in Jesus Christ, His only begotten Son, all fulness should dwell; wrapped up in Jesus was the fulness of God. Receive Him—and live. Reject Him—and you will spend eternity in the blackness of darkness forever!

Many have said to me, "I just cannot understand it!" I always reply, "Neither can I! I cannot understand the fulness of God, I cannot understand God's love; but I believe God loves me, I believe Christ died for me." We are not saved by understanding: *We are saved by faith in the finished work of the Lord Jesus Christ.* If I could understand God, if I could understand redemption, I would be as wise as the God who redeemed me—and I am so happy that my God is greater than I. His wisdom is far superior to human wisdom; His power is far greater than human power; and I am very willing to rest my case in His hands by faith. Do not forget: "The just shall live by faith." Stop trying to reason out spiritual things, and *believe them because God said them.*

PAUL WARNS AGAINST THE DANGER OF ENTICING WORDS

Verse 4: "And this I say, lest any man should beguile you with enticing words."

To paraphrase this verse of Scripture, Paul would say: "I am anxious for you, concerned about you; I love you with a deep love and I am saying this to put you on guard against the teachers of error, who are very capable from the standpoint of words—but fair, enticing words are not words that bring the new birth (I Peter 1:23), nor words that bring faith (Rom. 10:17), nor words that bring salvation (John 5:24). I say this in love: I do not want you to listen to the boasting of these teachers of error. They are not speaking pure wisdom, pure truth nor pure knowledge in keeping with what I have taught you, for they bypass the mystery which has been hidden in God from the beginning but which is now revealed, and they teach their own ideas concerning things pertaining to the spiritual world. The mystery that God revealed to me—and which I have revealed to you—contains all the treasures of wisdom and pure knowledge. Stand by what I have taught you and turn a deaf ear to the teachers of error."

False teachers—through great swelling words and high-sounding phrases—profess to bring to light the obscure. They do so by eliminating much of the truth and diluting the rest of truth with enticing phrases, seemingly making the obscure and the unknown more understandable; yet their teaching is gross error and spiritual poison. False teachers attempt to reconcile things that *seem* to be a discrepancy in the Bible. They point out certain phrases which may be a bit vague, and through their enticing words bring about reconciliation between what on the surface seem to be contradictions. They attempt to reason out things that are *beyond* reason. God is not found by searching nor by reason—but by naked faith. It is true that God tells us, "Come now, and let us reason together," but we cannot know Him through reason alone. We are not to *explain* God—we are to *trust* Him. In the words of Jesus to His disciples, we are to "have faith in God" (Mark 11:22).

In Colosse there were those who taught a form of mysticism which advertised communion with the invisible and the spiritual. Paul was greatly concerned that the believers steer clear of such teaching, and he knew the only way the Colossians could be victorious over these teachers of error was for them to have "full assurance of understanding" and the illuminating power of the Holy Spirit—thus accepting the true Gospel without question. If they possessed "the full assurance of understanding" they would not be led astray with enticing words, smooth language and the colorful phrases of the teachers of error.

Verse 5: "For though I be absent in the flesh, yet am I with you in the spirit, joying and beholding your order, and the stedfastness of your faith in Christ."

When God's minister takes a deep interest in a church or a group of believers and has in his heart a deep love for them, he is ever with them in spirit—and this is not mysticism or spiritualism. *In his heart* he is there—loving them, serving them, suffering with them. He is not there in body, he may not even be in their locality; but in his heart he walks with them, talks with them and dwells with them. He is a guest at their services even though he is not physically present.

So it was with Paul: He was in prison when he wrote this Epistle—but his heart was in Colosse. He was absent in body, but present in heart and spirit . . . "joying and beholding your order." Although imprisoned in body, mentally he was present with the believers at Colosse, rejoicing with them because of their love for all saints, because of their stewardship and because of their order. His spiritual presence with them was a deep source of joy even though he was behind bars, and this deep joy in the spirit enabled him to rejoice because of the consistency of the believers in the church at Colosse.

In chapter 1:3–4 he says that the reports received about their faithfulness and their love cause him, as often as he prays, to thank God for them, and in chapter 2:5 he assures them that even though imprisoned in body, he is rejoicing in spirit, that they are the source of his joy, and that he must, as their spiritual leader, warn them concerning the grave danger of falling into error.

Perhaps someone is wondering what Paul meant by the statement, "beholding your order." If we compare the Colossian believers with the church at Corinth we can understand what Paul means here: It seems that the Christians at Colosse did everything "decently and in order," but such was not true in the Corinthian church. If you will read Paul's epistles to the Corinthians you will discover that the Christians there were divided, they were fussing, they were misbehaving at the Lord's table. Various and sundry grievances were brought against them by the Apostle in his letters to them.

Also, in the church at Thessalonica Paul accuses certain members of walking "disorderly," and reminds them, "For we behaved not ourselves disorderly among you . . . for we hear that there are some which walk among you disorderly, working not at all, but are busybodies" (II Thess. 3:6,7,11). The disorderly conduct of the Thessalonians was the vicious tendency to idleness; they were lazy, refusing to labor to earn a livelihood.

Many of the brethren depended upon the liberality of the richer members of the church at Thessalonica and Paul condemned them for so doing. Read I Thessalonians 5:14. Paul admonished all believers, "Let all things be done decently and in order." In the churches at Thessalonica and Corinth there had been both social and ecclesiastical breach of order among the believers. Therefore, Paul commended the Colossians for their "good order."

Verse 5 closes with the words, ". . . and the stedfastness of your faith in Christ." The Greek word translated "stedfastness" is better translated "solidity," and it means "solid, or *compact.*" In other words, the Colossians had solid and stedfast faith. There were many noteworthy things about the believers at Colosse, but as Paul writes from the jail in Rome, the thing that stands out singularly in his mind is the unshaken faith of the true believers there. He was aware of their fruits, their love for all brethren, and their good order—but he rejoiced most in the solidity of their faith.

Note again: ". . . the stedfastness of your faith IN CHRIST." It was a distinguished and glorified faith because it reposed on Christ. The faith of the Colossians was *in the Christ* who could not be shaken or moved. His love never wavers nor changes; his power never fails, but is always the same. His Word is true, He cannot lie (Heb. 6:18; Titus 1:2). Every promise made by the Christ in whom the Colossians had faith is certain and sure and unfailing. Heaven's door is open to all who are in Christ. The everlasting stream of living water will never run dry for all who are in Christ. The Pearly Gates of that City will never close in the face of those who are in Christ, and the golden streets will be ever inviting the footsteps of all who walk by faith.

Verse 6: "As ye have therefore received Christ Jesus the Lord, so walk ye in Him."

In the previous verses, Paul has commended the believers for their order and their stedfastness in the faith; now he adds a word of warning and counsel. You will notice that in the Colossian letter Paul does not abruptly rebuke the Colossians concerning the teachers of error in their midst, but gradually approaches the subject and then minces no words in warning them concerning these deadly spiritualists. He assures them that if they have received Christ as Lord they should walk worthy of the Christ whom they have received.

Verse 6 sets forth the fact that the Colossians HAD already received Christ as Lord: ". . . as ye have therefore received Christ Jesus the Lord." Therefore, the anointed Jesus whom they had received is now to them "Lord of all." Since they had received Him as Lord, they should acknowledge His Lordship in every detail of life—both spiritual and secular—and should recognize His sovereign authority.

There are believers today who have received Jesus as Saviour but who have never acknowledged Him as Lord of all and have never permitted Him to become Lord of their life. In I Corinthians 12:3 Paul said to the believers at Corinth, "Wherefore I give you to understand, that no man speaking by the Spirit of God calleth Jesus accursed: and that *no man can say that Jesus is the Lord, but by the Holy Ghost.*" The outstanding error being taught in Colosse was error that robbed Jesus the Saviour of His divine dignity, robbed Him of His Messiahship in its true sense and full meaning and explained away His humanity, thereby making Him a spirit-being instead of the God-man.

This was a form of spiritualism—and we have the same error all around us today! We have teachers today who readily admit the historical character of Jesus Christ; they readily admit that He was a great man and quite extraordinary; *but they refuse to admit His deity*. Regardless of who the person is, any one who denies that Jesus was the God-man . . . that person is a false prophet, a minister of the devil, and his end will be in the lake of fire!

There is no such thing taught in the Bible as accepting *part* of Christ but not *all* of Christ. II John 7—11 gives a warning which many church people refuse to obey:

"For many deceivers are entered into the world, who confess not that Jesus Christ is come in the flesh. This is a deceiver and an antichrist. Look to yourselves, that we lose not those things which we have wrought, but that we receive a full reward. Whosoever transgresseth, and abideth not in the doctrine of Christ, hath not God. He that abideth in the doctrine of Christ, he hath both the Father and the Son. If there come any unto you, and bring not this doctrine, receive him not into your house, neither bid him God speed: For he that biddeth him God speed is partaker of his evil deeds."

In these verses John gives the same warning Paul gives to the Colossians. Many deceivers are entered into the world, and these deceivers confess not that Jesus Christ is come in the flesh. John tells us that any person who refuses to confess that Jesus Christ is God, and that He came in the flesh, that person is a deceiver and an antichrist. We are then warned to be careful and watch ourselves that we lose not our reward.

All believers are solemnly admonished that if any come and bring not *the doctrine of Christ*, that person does not have God. ("He that abideth IN the doctrine of Christ, He hath the Father and the Son.") But if any come and bring NOT this doctrine, do not invite him into your home and do not bid him God speed . . . that is, do not give him an offering, do not feed him, do not clothe him, do not afford him a place to sleep. Any person who denies God in the flesh *as Jesus*; any person who denies the Trinity; any person who denies the blood atonement, the virgin birth and the teachings of Jesus, is not to be bidden God speed by believers; for whosoever shall bid such a one God speed thereby becomes his co-laborer, his fellowworker, and a "partaker of his evil deeds." When a Christian supports a person who denies any part of the Gospel, that Christian is contributing to the damnation of souls—and that is a grave offence against Almighty God.

The paramount question today is, *"What think ye of Christ?"* Whatsoever men receive in the Gospel, it is because of Christ—the only begotten Son of God:

Christ is the beginning of all doctrine and the soul of all doctrine.

The prophets prophesied concerning Christ.

The apostles preached Christ, and Christ alone.

All truth originates in Christ: He IS the truth.

All hope rests in Christ, because if in this life only we have hope, we are of all men most miserable!

All ethical teaching has a close connection with Christ. Whatsoever we do, whatsoever we think, whatsoever we say, whatsoever we are, all should be to His honor and glory—and for His sake.

There is victory for the believer in Christ—and *only* in Christ: "Whosoever is born of God overcometh the world, and this is the victory that overcometh the world, even our faith." Christ is the author and finisher of our faith (Rom. 10:17; Heb. 12:1—3). Every promise in the Bible is based upon the finished work of the Lord Jesus Christ. He has never broken any promise spoken—but *there could be no promise fulfilled* had He not willingly laid His life down (John 10:18). Had He not willingly suffered, bled and died, all the promises from Genesis through Revelation would have been vain and empty.

Christ holds the destiny of all mankind in His hand. He is the hope of civilization, He is the beginning of all spiritual life. In Christ there is light, love, power, assurance, safety and security. He who was in the Father's bosom (John 1:18) left the Father's house and came to earth's sorrows, and in His own body bore our sins on His cross. He laid His life down, He was buried in a borrowed tomb, He walked out of the grave—and in one step passed from the sepulchre to the throne. He sits today at the right hand of God the Father, beholding the affairs of men. He who by Himself purged our sins, ascended to the Father and sat down at the right hand of God to make intercession for you and me . . . that is, those of us who, like the Colossians, have put our faith and trust in Him as Saviour and then willingly acknowledged Him as Lord of our lives (I Tim. 2:5; Heb. 1:1—3; I John 2:1,2).

Verse 6 closes with the solemn words, *"Walk ye in Him!"* The statement here is referring to manner of life and visible conduct. The Colossians had received Christ as Saviour—and since He was Saviour of their soul, the *least* they could do was permit Him to be Lord of their life and walk as though He walked by their side, observing their every movement throughout the hours of the day.

Paul wanted the believers at Colosse to know assuredly that they had received a Person—not a creed or a theme, but One who was there with them ("Christ in you, the hope of glory"); and since Christ had taken up His abode in their hearts, they should conduct themselves in their daily living as though He were visibly present with them every moment of the day.

That is the answer to the question, "Why do some church members walk as they walk?" A person cannot walk aright until Jesus Christ has been accepted in the heart. The reception of Jesus in the heart precedes holy living . . . the outer life demonstrates the *inner life.* The ability to walk right is the result of Christ in the Christian: "As many as are led by the Spirit of God, they are the children of God" (Rom. 8:14). If we walk in the Spirit we will not fulfill the lust of the flesh.

In Romans 8:1 we have this tremendous truth: "There is therefore now no condemnation to them which are in Christ Jesus, *who walk not after the flesh, but after the Spirit.*" The last part of that verse does not say, "IF they walk not after the flesh, but after the Spirit." Receiving Jesus automatically produces a righteous walk. Since the Colossians had received Him as Saviour they could not help walking in Him as Lord; to do anything less would be to deliberately deny what they had professed to believe and receive: namely, *the fulness of the Godhead in Christ Jesus.*

What Paul is saying here to the Colossians is simply that they should stand fast concerning what they had received in Christ Jesus. If they were tempted by the teachers of error to reject the qualifications of Christ in any way—however insignificant it might be—or if they in any way modified the teachings concerning His incarnation or set aside any one of His claims; if they attempted to deny or explain away His true humanity as Jesus the Saviour; if they attempted to deny the fact that He was God and yet man, thus placing Him in the mystical, spiritual realm instead of the reality of the incarnation; if they denied any minute detail of the fundamentals of the faith they would succumb to the teaching of error, thereby losing their power, joy and testimony.

What Paul commanded the Colossian believers to accept without reservation was the fact of the humanity of Jesus . . . the life of Jesus on earth in flesh . . . the reality that He was God in flesh, the fact of His atoning death and His bodily resurrection. They must not withhold their allegiance to Him as Lord of their life. They MUST have unshakeable faith in Him as the Christ of God—very God in flesh—reconciling the world unto Himself, and yet as Christ, the Brother of all believers, the Keeper and Preserver of all saints, the One who bestows all blessings upon the obedient ones. They must accept Him as Saviour and Lord because "He IS thy Lord. Worship thou Him!"

The true believer has life IN Christ and life FROM Christ. The things we do as true believers are determined, certainly to a great extent, because we know we are in His presence. If believers walk in Christ, they are fortified against doubts and against the dangerous teachings of error. Believers who walk in Christ have wisdom and the leadership of the Spirit which *insures them against the poison of error*: "Wherefore also it is contained in the Scripture, Behold, I lay in Sion a chief corner stone, elect, precious: and he that believeth on Him shall not be confounded (confused)" (I Peter 2:6).

The first desire of the devil is to damn you and see you burn in hell. If you hear the Gospel and trust the Lord Jesus Christ as Saviour, the devil knows he has lost you as a potential for damnation—but he does not give up. When you are born again, he declares war on you through false teachers and in many other ways, to rob you of the joy of your salvation, to rob you of the power of your testimony, and to defeat you in your spiritual living. It is one thing to be redeemed; it is quite another thing to be a surrendered, fruit-bearing Christian. It is one thing to enter Heaven; it is another thing to receive "a full reward." Some will be snatched "as a brand from the burning." Some will see their works burned and they will suffer loss, while still others will stand before Jesus *"ashamed."*

Verse 7: "Rooted and built up in Him, and stablished in the faith, as ye have been taught, abounding therein with thanksgiving."

Bible scholars who are authorities on Greek tell us that the wording here is used "in a topical sense." The ideas set forth are stability and growth, rooted in Jesus— established, immoveable, stable—and *growing.* Since believers are ROOTED IN HIM there is no possibility of eradication of life. In Him we live and move and have our being as sons of God. To destroy the life of a believer it would be necessary for the devil to destroy Him in whom we are rooted! The believer IN HIM has an unshaken and unshakeable foundation.

In John 15 we read, "I am the Vine, ye are the branches." Every believer is connected to the vine; the life of the branch comes from the vine. IN HIM we have life (we are saved); out of Christ we have no life (we are lost). The term "rooted" indicates a previous transaction, and the statement "built up in Him" signifies a present condition in the life of the believer. All believers are *rooted* (past tense), but we are to GROW in grace, to become strong in the Lord and press toward the mark of the high calling of God in Christ Jesus. Believers are to be making progress if they are in the center of God's will.

What Paul is attempting to instill in the hearts of believers is the fact that we are rooted in Christ, we are baptized into His body, we are hid with Christ in God, we are sealed with the Holy Ghost until the day of redemption. Believers are not simply adhering to Him by some superficial tie of religion or man-made dogma; we are connected to Him, being built up in Him because we are members of His body—bone of His bone, flesh of His flesh (Eph. 5:30). Therefore, the Colossians were to defy all endeavors on the part of the teachers of error

114

to lead them astray from the truth. *Jesus is the truth* (John 14:6; 17:17).

Paul admonished the believers at Colosse to be "stablished in the faith as ye have been taught." They were to be confirmed in the faith which had been taught them by Paul—and also by Epaphras and the faithful leaders in the church. Paul wanted them to have strong faith, *overflowing faith*; they were to *abound* in faith. May God help you and me to recognize the solemn fact that He honors faith! We are *saved by grace* through faith, *the just* shall *live* by faith, and *whatsoever is not of faith is sin.* We are admonished to be not faith-*less*, but *believing.*

All believers should always be "abounding therein with thanksgiving"; thus closes verse 7. True believers cannot help being thankful that they have heard the truth, that they have been brought to a knowledge of the truth, and that by divine power and the grace of God they have accepted the truth. There are thousands of dear people in our country—and millions throughout the world—who have never been exposed to real Gospel truth. They were born into homes and families where cults and false religions have been practiced for generations. In many cases they are forbidden to attend fundamental churches, forbidden to listen to radio broadcasts or read fundamental literature; therefore they are cut off from the light. It is true that occasionally one of these people will hear the Gospel and be saved, but the vast majority of those who have been brought up in religions of darkness instead of the truth will die in darkness and spend eternity in hell. Paul admonished the believers at Colosse to be thankful that they had heard the truth, and that they had unreservedly accepted that truth.

Verse 7 is both precept and warning, and if the believers at Colosse obeyed the precept and heeded the

115

warning, those who taught "philosophy and vain deceit" would find their message falling on deaf ears in the Colossian community. Again and again thus far in the Epistle to the Colossians, Paul has approached the main subject of the Epistle by indirect allusions. Now he boldly brings out the real issue . . . the number one reason for his writing:

Verse 8: "Beware lest any man spoil you through philosophy and vain deceit, after the tradition of men, after the rudiments of the world, and *not after Christ.*"

Some have suggested that Paul was against the study of philosophy and science; that he was against a person's attempting to increase his knowledge and wisdom concerning the universe and all things pertaining thereto: but not so. Paul was a scholar . . . a learned man. He sat at the feet of Gamaliel, the most outstanding teacher of that day. Philosophy, science, or the pursuit and love of wisdom cannot be stigmatized as being in itself hostile to faith. Paul himself employed philosophy to prove the existence of Jehovah God and show the foolishness and folly of the sin of idolatry. In Romans 1:19–23 Paul sets forth an argument, and then in Romans 2:1 he thunders out, *"Thou art inexcusable, O man!"*

We live in a marvelous universe. Wherever we look— whether we look upon ourselves or *beyond* ourselves— we see a thousand things that invite our study and examination. The more thoroughly we study and examine them, the more thoroughly we are convinced that there is an eternal Creator behind all creation. These things did not "just happen."

In the glorious lights of the heavens above us, we can see the shadow of God's divine countenance. When we look around us and see God's goodness to His creatures, we recognize immediately God's manifold goodness.

No wonder the Psalmist thundered out, "The fool hath said in his heart, There is no God!"

"The heavens declare the glory of God; and the firmament sheweth His handywork. Day unto day uttereth speech, and night unto night sheweth knowledge. There is no speech nor language, where their voice is not heard" (Psalm 19:1–3).

To the Romans Paul said, "For the wrath of God is revealed from heaven against all ungodliness and unrighteousness of men, who hold the truth in unrighteousness; Because that which may be known of God is manifest in them; for God hath shewed it unto them. For the invisible things of Him from the creation of the world are clearly seen, being understood by the things that are made, even His eternal power and Godhead; so that *they are without excuse*" (Rom. 1:18–20).

One outstanding scholar defines philosophy as "acquaintance with divine and human things." Philosophy can be beneficial. The more a man knows about himself and the more he knows about his own nature, the more deeply he will feel his need of God and the more he will understand that he is created in the image of a divine God, in order that God may communicate with man and man with God. These bodies of ours are marvelous beyond words. For example—who fully understands the eye? It is fitted for the reception of light, and light alone can make it possible for the eye to fulfill its functions in the human body.

In the same manner, true Gospel truth alone is fitted to satisfy the yearnings, longings and hunger of the human heart. Perfect harmony can be found between God and man if man will rely fully and entirely upon the truth of God. God created man after such a fashion that no man can be happy, no man can be at peace nor enjoy

117

life fully until he is in the right relationship with his Creator—Almighty God.

To accept wrong belief and gross error *in the light of clear Scripture* is certainly against reason. To read the account of creation in the Word of God, to read of the origin of man and the sacrifice of Jesus on the cross for remission of sin—and then to manufacture one's own belief about these clearly stated facts is certainly unreasonable: but to read the Word of God with an open mind and an open heart and then say, *"I do not believe it,"* is not only unreasonable—it also is against nature! God so created man that it is natural for him to feel his need of One greater than himself. Regardless of where we may go on this earth, we will find that men worship some kind of god—even in heathen lands where they have never heard the Gospel and know nothing of the truth.

After reading the Word of God with an open heart, a sound philosophy comes to this conclusion: In Christianity there is found every need supplied. In Christianity we find God our Creator incarnate in Jesus Christ our Saviour. True Christianity reveals the shed blood, the atonement, the redemption Jesus alone could and did purchase willingly for sinners (John 10:18; I Peter 1: 18—20). Christianity satisfies the longing of the heart for existing time and gives hope to the heart for eternity . . . looking beyond life into heaven, knowing that the God who created us and provided redemption for us will surely keep every promise to us!

As I have already stated, man is so created that he must have some kind of god; he is always seeking something beyond himself—some revelation. Christianity gives to man the true God and reveals to him the truth which makes men free. Man depends upon some form of sacrifice to satisfy his conscience; Christianity reveals the Perfect Sacrifice—offered once, for all, forever—never to be offered again: *the blood of Jesus Christ.* Man anticipates something after his sojourn here on earth; Christianity assures him that there IS a home beyond the stars, and teaches him how to reach that heavenly home. Jesus said, "Ye shall know the truth, and the truth shall make you free. . . . If the Son therefore shall make you free, ye shall be free indeed" (John 8:32,36).

A little later He said to His disciples, "I am going to Jerusalem. There I will be arrested, tried, convicted, condemned and crucified." Their hearts were broken; Thomas asked, "We know not whither thou goest, and how can we know the way?" In answer to this question Jesus said, "I am the Way, the Truth, and the Life. No man cometh unto the Father but by me" (John 14:1-6). In Christ we have hope and assurance, we find peace that surpasses all understanding, and "he that believeth on Him shall not be confused" (John 14:27; I Peter 2:6).

Paul does not here condemn such philosophy. Philosophy in the beginning was a generous, noble thing; a virgin beauty, a pure light, born of the Father of lights (James 1:17). However, we must face the fact that the greater portion of heresies have been and are today allied to some type of a false philosophy. Christianity since its birth has suffered from four outstanding forms of philosophy:

1. Sensationalism
2. Idealism
3. Skepticism
4. Mysticism

The error of each of these philosophies lies in the fact that men have pushed some important fundamental truth beyond reason and to extravagance. The devil tempted Jesus with sensationalism; he put Him on the pinnacle of the temple and invited Him to cast Himself down,

119

assuring Him that the angels would take care of Him (Matt. 4:5,6). He would have been very sensational— but He did not come into this world to be sensational; He came to be the Saviour of sinners.

The philosophy against which Paul warned the Colossians was a philosophy that developed superstition in the mind and crossed the path of the Gospel. It did not deal with nature *around* it, but with the supernatural *beyond* it. It was a philosophy that lived in a spirit-world which it had created. Such philosophy did not accept the Apostolic Faith of Christianity, and the truths of Christianity did not satisfy the appetites of those who preached this doctrine. It went beyond the manifold wisdom of the cross of the Lord Jesus. It was not satisfied to accept the pure Gospel as the final truth concerning salvation by grace through faith in the finished work of the Lord Jesus and the fact that we are complete in Him— *plus nothing*. This was the false philosophy and error that Paul so earnestly begged the Colossians to be on guard against, lest anyone spoil them and rob them of their spiritual birthright.

Paul was jealous for Jesus; he was against anything that was "not after Christ." He wanted the Colossians to do all things IN Christ, *to the glory of Christ* and *in the name of Christ*. The philosophy set forth by the teachers of error was made up of vain words and "vain deceit"; there was no reality in what they taught. Such teaching was "after the tradition of men" and not according to the divine revelation of the Gospel.

In that day the Jews had added a great many oral teachings to the written law. Many of these teachings were old, having been handed down from generation to generation, and thus they had added to "the commands of God." It was solely of man, and partook largely of his vanity and weakness. Some of the teachers of that day were fanatical concerning some parts of the Law. They taught the payment of "mint, anise and cummin"— but after screaming long and loud concerning the tithe and the gross sin committed by those who did not tithe, they omitted "the weightier matters of the law," such as judgment, mercy and faith. They became very much alarmed when the disciples ate without washing their hands—but they refused to hear the teachings of Jesus concerning regeneration and the new birth which afforded a clean heart. They taught that the outside of the cup should be very clean—but they backed away from the teaching of a clean heart and a clean conscience. They rejoiced in the labors of their own hands, they were sticklers for the Law and the tradition of the fathers; but they had neither time nor place for "the sacrifice of a broken and a contrite heart."

One of the most subtle and damning errors of our day and hour is that men who profess to be religious leaders and representatives of the Gospel refuse to permit the Gospel to have the final word; they are forever adding their own interpretation. They add to and take from the plain Gospel of salvation by grace through faith in the finished work of Jesus. They announce grace— and preach works. They announce the Gospel—and preach the traditions of men. They announce allegiance to God— and yet seek to please the denomination or the religious leaders in their group, and by so doing commit the same sin as the preachers of error in Colosse committed in deviating from the Gospel of Grace and mixing the traditions of men, Judaism, spiritualism and other "isms" in an attempt to lead the Colossians away from pure grace and the finished work of the Lamb of God.

The phrase "after the rudiments of the world" no doubt refers to Jewish worship. In Galatia the believers were strongly tempted to either revert to Judaism or incorporate Judaism (in part) into the new religion they had received through Paul's preaching of the Gospel. They seemed inclined to cling to ceremonies and types. We will discuss this a bit further in later verses of the chapter.

During the transition period it was very difficult for believers to completely break away from Judaism. Even today men flock to religions of works, ceremonies, days and images. Human nature craves to SEE something or FEEL something—but Christianity cries out, *"The just shall live by faith!"*

It is true that we do not know all of the error being taught in Colosse; we cannot define it fully; but we know that it was not "after Christ." Paul cried out against anything that demoted Christ or took away from Him. Christ is the center of Christianity; Christ is the center of true philosophy and the center of true science. The fear of the Lord is the beginning of knowledge, and the very essence of true knowledge is Jesus Christ. If any man lack wisdom, "let him ask of God, who giveth to all men liberally." "Christ is made unto us WISDOM, RIGHTEOUSNESS, SANCTIFICATION, AND REDEMPTION."

Before leaving this verse, let me point out one thing more: These preachers of error did not come in boldly as did the Judaizers in Galatia; they were much more subtle and more insidious in their poisonous attack upon the truth. They did not publicly announce that the Gentile believers must be circumcised and keep the Law— it would have been much better if they had, for then they would have been confronted like the Judaizers in Galatia. But these teachers were more cunning in their attack. They boasted that they possessed a deeper experience, a higher knowledge, and preached an ideal system made up apparently of Judaism and Gnosticism. Paul knew that if the Colossian believers listened to the teachers of error, they would lose their power, their testimony, their reward—and souls would be damned because of it.

COMPLETENESS
Nothing Can Be Added

Verse 9: *"For in Him dwelleth all the fulness of the Godhead bodily."* After the warning of verse 8, the truth set forth in verse 9 is an undeniable, irresistable argument that any system or teaching or doctrine that is not after Christ is certainly human, man-made, and grossly wrong. IN HIM (Christ) dwells all the fulness of the Godhead bodily.

Greek authorities tell us that the truth set forth in the language of verse 9 declares that in Jesus is found all the attributes of the Godhead—the whole, the fullness; not just part, or partial possession . . . not part of the glories of the Godhead nor a measure of the power of the Godhead . . . but in Jesus dwells *all the fullness* that constitutes divinity and sovereign God. What can be added? Who would dare attempt the addition of anything to the fullness of the Godhead? Yet in Paul's day— as in our own—there were men who were teaching such a philosophy.

All who will accept the Word of God without attempting to prove a religion, a dogma or doctrine, can readily see that verse 9 clearly teaches that Jesus was the fullness of the Godhead. The Godhead assumed a bodily form in Jesus; He was the visible shape in which the fullness of the Godhead dwelt, and men beheld His glory — the glory of the only begotten of the Father. The Godhead in its fullness took up abode in Christ as a man . . . took up residence in humanity—the humanity of Jesus, born of the virgin Mary. Divinity was incarnate in Christ.

The coming Saviour was described with the prophetic title, "Emmanuel, *God with us*" (Matt. 1:23). John gives us the same truth in John 1:1 and 14: "In the beginning was the Word, and the Word was with God, and the Word was God . . . *and the Word was made flesh and dwelt among us.*"

I realize that the truth set forth in verse 9 is too wonderful for the finite mind of man to fully grasp. I confess that it is beyond my understanding—yet I believe it! Read slowly, study carefully—and you will appreciate the Saviour more than you ever have. *The Word* was in the beginning with Jehovah, sovereign God; the Word was unfleshed (without body); *the Word was God*. According to the Holy Spirit's revelation to John, the Word was with God, the Word was divine—yet definitely distinct from the Father.

In the fullness of time (Gal. 4:4) the Word took up its abode in humanity (flesh), the miracle being that the Word became flesh without *consuming* flesh, and without *altering* flesh insofar as its essential properties and habits are concerned. The Word (God) that was in the beginning *with* God, in the bosom of the Father, took flesh—and in that body ate as all men eat, became thirsty as all men become thirsty; grieved, shed tears, prayed, became weary, lay down in a little ship and slept—so exhausted that a raging storm did not disturb or waken Him. Finally, the Word (in flesh) died on a cross—willingly, voluntarily—that we might live! The incarnation is truly a divine miracle—God in flesh!

God gave the Word a body—and in that body Jesus tasted death for every man (Heb. 2:9). In that body of flesh He met and conquered him who had the keys of hell and death. In the words of the Spirit as Paul penned them down, Jesus Himself "took part of the same (flesh); that through death He might destroy him that had the power of death, that is, the devil; and deliver them who through fear of death were all their lifetime subject to bondage. For verily He took not on Him the nature of angels; but He took on Him the seed of Abraham" (Heb. 2:14–16).

In the day of Paul, in the community of the Colossians there were those who refused to accept the truth that Jesus was God-and-man in one body . . . a body of flesh just as surely as you and I are flesh. Jesus Christ—He who walked the shores of Galilee and ministered to all who came to Him—did not possess the nature of angels. He was not a spirit-being like the cherubim. He, like "the children of men," took part of man—the flesh part—a body. God sent His own Son "in the likeness of sinful flesh" (Rom. 8:1–3). He was born of a virgin; He was born exactly as the children of men are born, with the exception of the fact that the virgin Mary was His mother and God Almighty was His Father. The Holy Ghost overshadowed Mary (Luke 1), she conceived and brought forth a Son. He was born as we were born; He was wrapped in swaddling clothes and laid in a manger. He grew as any normal child would grow . . . in wisdom and in physical stature . . . and in that human body the fullness of the Godhead dwelt.

During the earthly sojourn of Jesus His divine glory appeared through His earthly covering of flesh on many occasions. The radiance of divine glory was veiled—but it was not entirely shut off from the eyes of mortal men. His disciples "beheld His glory, the glory of the only begotten of the Father, full of grace and truth" (John 1:14). Peter was impressed tremendously by the glory in Jesus, and confessed his own exceeding sinfulness. Thomas cried out, "My Lord and my God!"

During the earthly ministry of Jesus, on many occasions He prayed for others—sometimes spending all

125

night in prayer—but not one time did He ask others to pray for HIM. When weary sinners fell at His feet, He never rebuked them nor said, "See thou do it not!" He did not chide, but rather forgave the woman who in penitent humility washed His feet with her tears and dried them with the hairs of her head. He never felt it to be idolatry on their part to offer Him homage, or that it was "robbery" to accept their humble position at His feet, for *He was God* in flesh. Paul describes His second coming as "the glorious appearing of the great God" (Titus 2:11–13).

John the Baptist was having successful evangelistic campaigns and was baptizing many. One day Jesus came to him for baptism and John, knowing that Jesus was no ordinary person, "forbade Him saying, I have need to be baptized of thee," but Jesus said, "Suffer it to be so now: for thus it becometh us to fulfill all righteousness." When John baptized Jesus, a literal voice from heaven spoke: "This is my beloved Son, in whom I am well pleased" (Matt. 3:17).

On the Mount of Transfiguration, where the greatest Bible Conference ever held took place, Peter and the other disciples slept, awakening just in time for the benediction—and Peter never got over it. More than thirty years later when he wrote the Epistle that bears his name, he said, "We have not followed cunningly devised fables. We were eyewitnesses of His majesty" (II Peter 1:16). Jesus knew the inmost thoughts and the intent of His enemies; He knew the heartbeat of the multitude, for He possessed a species of knowledge which is far above humanity. He knew all men, because He knew what was in man (John 2:25).

Jesus claimed to be God—and He proved it by the things He did while here on earth in the flesh. In a wind-tossed ship on a stormy sea, when His disciples cried,

126

"Carest thou not that we perish?" Jesus spoke a simple "Peace, be still!" and the angry winds ceased to blow. He made a sidewalk of the waters of the Sea of Galilee, walking upon them as if they were of concrete. He overstepped all the laws of medicine, science—and even the Mosaic Law concerning the leper—for He touched the leper and made him clean, instead of Himself becoming a leper from that touch.

The eye of the most ordinary person who saw Jesus had no trouble discovering that there was something extraordinary about Him; even His enemies admitted that they had "never seen it on this fashion," and when the religious leaders of the day heard Him teach they admitted that He spake "as One having authority, and not as the scribes."

After He had conducted street meetings where people were saved and healed of all kinds of diseases, the spectators agreed, "We have seen strange things today." The God-man, Christ, demonstrated power and perfection not known to earthly creatures; His very nature testified to His divinity. The devil and his demons, who find it so easy to lead mankind astray, could not cause THE HOLY ONE OF GOD to sin in either thought, word or deed. On every occasion He answered the prince of this world with the Word of God, and the demons readily confessed that He was the Son of the living God! The demons (and even the devil himself) had—and still have—more respect for the Son of God than do some preachers in American pulpits today!

The Man in whom Paul declared "dwelleth all the fulness of the Godhead bodily" was the image of the invisible God, and so close was His likeness to the eternal God who sent Him, that He said to one of His disciples, "HE THAT HATH SEEN ME HATH SEEN THE FATHER!" In clear, unmistakeable terms the Apostle

127

Paul affirms, in this brief but tremendously weighty clause, the great mystery of Christ's mediatorial nature—the personal union in Him of divinity (yea, very God) and manhood (flesh), even "the likeness of *sinful* flesh."

Without apology Paul declares that any philosophy that is not "AFTER CHRIST" is earthly, devilish, deceitful—and gross error, missing the central truth, the center of God's eternal program: the Son of the living God, in whom dwells all the fullness of the Godhead bodily.

Verse 10: *"And ye are complete in Him,* which is the head of all principality and power."

With these words Paul reminds us that nothing can be added to the finished work of the Son of God; and nothing can be added to grace: It is grace—ALL grace, or NO grace. Believers are complete in the Lord Jesus. (The word *complete* has the same meaning as *perfect*— so what Paul is really saying is, *"Ye are perfect in Him."*) Believers have now (present tense) fullness, spiritual perfection, the righteousness of God, and justification. "Christ is made unto us wisdom, righteousness, sanctification and redemption." We have the wisdom of Christ; we have the sanctification of Christ; we have the redemption He purchased with His own precious blood.

One who has truly believed, who has exercised true faith, has the divine guarantee of completeness in Christ: "Ye ARE complete in Him" . . . not "WILL be complete (at some future date)," but "ARE complete (present tense)." In Christ nothing is lacking. Every need, no matter how great nor how small, is met in Christ. What God demands, He has provided in the finished work of the Son of His love.

In the last part of verse 10 Paul refers to the Christ— "which is the Head of all principality and power." The deep meaning of verse 10 is thus: In Christ—and that bodily—is found and dwells all the Godhead's fullness, which is the head of all principalities and all powers. There is no exception; the entire hierarchy of heaven must submit to Christ because He is above all; there is none higher in heaven, in earth nor under the earth. Therefore, inasmuch as He is the all-powerful One, He is very able to supply complete salvation, complete forgiveness, complete righteousness. To put it in Bible language, "Ye are complete in Him!"

Verse 11: "In whom also ye are circumcised with the circumcision made without hands, in putting off the body of the sins of the flesh by the circumcision of Christ."

Let me call your attention to the words "In whom . . . in Him . . . of Christ . . . with Him." In other words—CHRIST. Paul's singular subject was Christ for all things, because in Him is completeness. Therefore, because the Colossians were in Christ through the miracle of faith in His finished work, they possessed and enjoyed the privileges that are the results of spiritual circumcision "not made with hands." Why then should such privileged sons of God return to the things of the flesh? to the ordinances of men? The circumcision made without hands is clearly opposed to that which is made with man's hands (Eph. 2:11).

The doctrine of spiritual circumcision as declared by Paul was not a new doctrine; it occurs many times in the Old Testament in different forms. When Israel was yet in the wilderness the divine *command* from Almighty God was given: "Circumcise the foreskin of your *heart*"; and at the same time, the divine *promise* was given: "And the Lord thy God will circumcise thine heart, and the heart of thy seed, to love the Lord thy God with all of thine heart and with all of thy soul, that thou mayest live."

To God's chosen people, Jeremiah gave the command, "Circumcise yourselves to the Lord, and take away the foreskins of your heart, ye men of Judah and inhabitants of Jerusalem . . ." (Jer. 4:4). Jeremiah describes the hard-hearted people thus: "Behold their ear is uncircumcised." Speaking of the whole house of Israel, he cried out that they were "uncircumcised in the heart."

Ezekiel declared the same in these words: "Uncircumcised in heart and uncircumcised in flesh." Stephen used the same words in his sermon to the Pharisees: "Ye uncircumcised in heart and ears" (Acts 7:51). Paul sometimes uses similar language when referring to hard-hearted and hard-of-hearing believers. There is a circumcision of heart that is made without hands, which provides invaluable blessings and indescribable glory to those who receive by faith the fullness of God in Christ Jesus. Read Deuteronomy 10:16; 30:6; Jeremiah 4:4; 6:10; 9:26; Ezekiel 44:7.

The circumcision not made with hands but "by Christ" brings about "putting off the body of the sins of the flesh." (Flesh here denotes corrupted humanity—Romans 7:23; Galatians 5:16; Ephesians 2:2.) Man is totally depraved and the body of flesh is hopelessly incurable. Paul contrasts here the circumcision of the flesh with the circumcision of Christ: Circumcision as having to do with the Law of Moses was limited, whereas circumcision in Christ *puts away the entire body of the flesh* and we are no longer in the flesh but in the Spirit: "But ye are not in the flesh, but in the Spirit, if so be that the Spirit of God dwell in you. Now if any man have not the Spirit of Christ, he is none of His" (Rom. 8:9).

Spiritual circumcision is not separate from regeneration . . . it is one and the same. Spiritual circumcision is not a second work of grace nor an added work of grace . . . it occurs when we are made new through the miracle of the new birth: "If any man be in Christ, He is a new creature: old things are passed away; behold, all things are become new" (II Cor. 5:17).

Paul gives us a further explanation of this marvelous change by saying, ". . . by the circumcision of Christ." Jesus said, "Think not that I am come to destroy the law, or the prophets: I am not come to destroy, but to fulfil" (Matt. 5:17). Paul adds, "Christ is the end of the law for righteousness to everyone that believeth" (Rom. 10:4). Therefore the circumcision of Christ is that circumcision which belongs to Him, provided only by and through His finished work; and is far, far greater than that circumcision which belonged to the Law of Moses. "The law came by Moses—but grace and truth came by Jesus Christ." Spiritual circumcision is a singular blessing which can be given only by the Christ in whom dwells all the fullness of the Godhead bodily, and in whom abide all the wells of salvation with their blessings.

Circumcision as having to do with the Law of Moses declared that the Hebrew manchild, at the age of eight days, was to be circumcised—thus identifying him with God's chosen people; but the circumcision in Christ is the privilege of all—there is no distinction, there is no age limit, sex or nation. It belongs to "whosoever will." Everyone is included, not one is excluded. Christ fulfilled the Law, thus becoming the end of the Law to all who believe; therefore, when man truly believes on the Lord Jesus Christ, he is dead to the Law and the Law is dead to Him. If such a marvelous collection of spiritual blessings and benefits can be had by trusting in the finished work of Jesus, why should anyone entertain the idea of becoming again subject to legal ceremonies, rituals, days, feasts—and the Law?

Surely if the believers at Colosse had experienced

the miracle of the new birth by faith in the finished work of Jesus; if they possessed Christ in their hearts (the hope of glory), then why should they entertain the idea of returning to a sign . . . a figure . . . when they had the *living Christ* within their hearts? He had brought—not a figure, not a sign—but *true light and life* to all who had believed in His finished work.

One of the most difficult things on earth for any minister of the Gospel to do is bring people to the place where they are willing to *"let go, and let God."* Man wants to do something, give something, live something, or be something; he is not willing to confess his total depravity, his helpless, hopeless condition—and then fling himself literally at the feet of Jesus in submission to God.

Verse 12: "Buried with Him in baptism, wherein also ye are risen with Him through the faith of the operation of God, who hath raised Him from the dead."

The Greek reads, ". . . *having been buried* with Him in baptism." Thus, *having been buried* with Christ in baptism, they were circumcised in Christ—not in the flesh, but in the Spirit. A new heart, a new spirit, a new life was theirs—a present possession in Christ. When a true believer undergoes true baptism and is immersed in water according to the New Testament formula, that person is thereby testifying to a previous death—such death having occurred when the person being baptized believed on the Lord Jesus Christ with the heart.

The moment a sinner believes on Jesus and receives His finished work, that same moment that person dies to sin. Baptism denotes burial to the body of sin. When we accept the finished work of Jesus Christ for remission of sin, we accept His death, burial and resurrection. There was no instrument used in the circumcision referred

132

to by Paul ("not with hands") and in like manner, when he refers to baptism as a burial, there is no shroud or bier used when the burial takes place. True baptism occurs the moment one believes: "For by one Spirit are we all baptized into one body, whether we be Jews or Gentiles, whether we be bond or free" (I Cor. 12:13).

Water baptism is a visible demonstration of an invisible miracle within. What Paul is saying to the Colossians here is simply this: "When you were baptized you testified that old things had passed away. Through your baptism you testified that you had died to the flesh, that you were done with the flesh." Certainly we know that not all people who are baptized are born again; many people who have been immersed in water bear no fruits of salvation whatsoever. Paul said, "All are not Israel who are of Israel," and in the same manner it is true that all are not truly born again who profess to have been baptized into the New Testament Church. But notice—this burial is not final:

"Wherein also ye are risen with Him through the faith of the operation of God who hath raised Him from the dead." Paul here has reference to the ordinance of baptism and the deep spiritual meaning it holds for the true believer. *The act of baptism* by putting one under the water certainly does not produce the death or the burial; nor does the *raising out of the water* produce resurrection to newness of life. The death, burial and resurrection are spiritual truths *portrayed* by baptism; but true death, true burial and true resurrection are experienced in the heart.

Verse 12 climaxes with a very important statement: "Ye are risen with Him THROUGH THE FAITH OF THE OPERATION OF GOD." Therefore, it is not the water in the baptistry or the river which achieves this spiritual resurrection; it is faith—faith in the divine program of

133

God which was settled before the foundation of the world (I Peter 1:18–23). Faith in the finished work of Jesus is the vehicle (or the wherewithal) through which the divine resurrection takes place. Water in baptism has nothing whatsoever to do with regeneration.

In Ephesians 1:19–20 Paul prays that the believers at Ephesus might know "what is the *exceeding greatness of God's power* to us-ward WHO BELIEVE." The power to which Paul is referring in this passage is the power of God that raised up Christ from the dead, and which also quickens (or makes alive) all who believe in the finished work of Jesus. Those who are "dead in trespasses and sins" (Eph. 2:1,2) are made alive through faith. "By grace are ye saved through faith; and that not of yourselves: it is the gift of God" (Eph. 2:8).

". . . THE FAITH OF THE OPERATION OF GOD, who hath raised Him from the dead." Truly, *salvation is of the Lord*. All are born in sin and shapen in iniquity. Man is totally depraved and he cannot save himself. The unbeliever must be raised out of spiritual death and united to the body of Christ by the Holy Ghost (John 3:5; I Cor. 12:12,13). This can happen only by faith in God (we are justified by faith); and when we are justified by faith we are exempt from the penalty of the Law, because "Christ is the end of the law for righteousness to every one that believeth" (Rom. 10:4).

Believers are sanctified in Christ (I Cor. 1:30).

Believers possess divine nature (II Peter 1:4).

Believers possess the image of God, spiritually—and in the first resurrection will receive a glorified body just like the glorious resurrection body of Jesus (I John 3:1,2).

The resurrection of the spiritually dead soul is the work of omnipotence, totally and entirely of God. In the sweet by-and-by these mortal bodies will be changed—

and that, too, will be through the power of omnipotence! God loved sinners. Love may pity, love may feel sympathy for one who is in desperate need—but love in such cases may not go any further because of other limitations. BUT GOD NOT ONLY LOVED—*God had the power* to resurrect dead sinners and give them new life in Christ Jesus . . . Paul calls it "exceeding great and mighty power." Faith does not ask for explanations; faith simply accepts what God says *because* God *said it!*

The greatest bombshell ever to explode in the face of an unbelieving world was the resurrection of the Lord Jesus Christ—the one thing that was utterly impossible for the enemies of Jesus to explain away. The resurrection of Jesus proves beyond a shadow of a doubt God's acceptance of His atonement. God the Father raised His Son from the dead "and gave Him glory; that our faith and hope might be in God" (I Peter 1:21). The resurrection of Jesus Christ opened the door of salvation to "whosoever will," for Jesus satisfied every demand of God's Law and thus the majesty of the Law was vindicated.

God's Law is holy and the breaking of that Law is sin. *All have sinned* and come short of the glory of God; by the deeds of the Law there shall be no flesh justified. The wages of sin is death—therefore the Law demands death for the offender. But Jesus Christ took a body, His blood was shed, He willingly laid His life down and entered the tomb—but the tomb could not hold Him; His power brought Him forth again from the dead.

Jesus satisfied the Law that could have crushed and destroyed you and me. Since Jesus fulfilled every jot and tittle of the Law and the prophets, God can be just and merciful toward us, and the power that could have crushed us now lifts us from the mire of sin and quickens us, making us alive unto God through the power of the Spirit. In the finished work of Jesus, God the

135

Father is highly pleased: "He shall see of the travail of His soul and shall be satisfied."

Verse 13: "And you, being dead in your sins and the uncircumcision of your flesh, hath He quickened together with Him, having forgiven you all trespasses."

In this verse Paul appeals to the Colossian believers, desiring that they realize their present possession in Christianity. The quickening and raising from spiritual deadness have already been experienced and are now to be enjoyed. Life in Christ is not a blessing to be enjoyed only beyond the grave, but NOW. Paul does not say that believers soon will die—and when they are raised from the grave and given new bodies they will *then* enjoy eternal life and the blessings of spiritual life; he appeals to them to enjoy the spiritual birthright already conferred upon them through the divine power of God because they have accepted the Lord Jesus by faith. Before they trusted Jesus they were truly dead spiritually; but now they are just as truly alive unto God—not "*going to be* alive," but a present possession, "Christ in you" NOW. "There is therefore NOW no condemnation to them which are in Christ Jesus."

Paul referred to this spiritual deadness as "dead in your sins and the uncircumcision of your flesh," and then explained that Christians have been quickened together with Jesus and all trespasses are forgiven. Jesus does not forgive up to a point—and then supplement that forgiveness with works or law; He forgives ALL trespasses. Some of the Colossians wanted their flesh to bear the seal of the Abrahamic covenant for circumcision of the flesh as taught by the Law; the teachers of error in Colosse were overbearing in insisting on circumcision after the manner of the Law. Many believing Jews were very zealous of the Law during the days of transition and Paul had a difficult task in persuading these believers

136

that salvation is by grace—and *only grace.*

In writing to the Romans Paul clearly sets forth the fundamental truth that the Law could not save: "By the deeds of the law there shall no flesh be justified in His sight" (Rom. 3:20). "There is therefore now no condemnation to them which are in Christ Jesus, who walk not after the flesh, but after the Spirit. For the law of the Spirit of life in Christ Jesus hath made me free from the law of sin and death. FOR WHAT THE LAW COULD NOT DO, IN THAT IT WAS WEAK THROUGH THE FLESH, God sending His own Son in the likeness of sinful flesh, and for sin, condemned sin in the flesh: THAT THE RIGHTEOUSNESS of the law might be fulfilled in us, who walk not after the flesh, but after the Spirit" (Rom. 8:1–4).

What Paul is, saying to the Colossians in verse 13 is this: "God brought you to life together with Christ; He raised up Christ from the dead, and by the same power He raises dead sinners when they believe on the Lord Jesus." "And you hath He quickened, who were dead in trespasses and sins . . . even when we were dead in sins, (He) hath quickened us together *with Christ,* (by grace ye are saved)" (Eph. 2:1,5).

Verse 13 closes with the glorious declaration ". . . having *forgiven you all trespasses."* Of those who add Law to grace, let me ask: "On what mission did Jesus come into the world? Was it not to purchase our redemption?" The answer, of course, is: Yes, Jesus came on a singular mission to satisfy the Law of God, the righteousness of God, the holiness of God, in order that God could be just and yet justify the believing sinner.

Just before Jesus committed His spirit to the Father He said, "It is finished." Nothing can be added to that which is finished. Eternal life is God's gift (Eph. 2:8).

A gift that is *a gift indeed* has no strings attached. We are not saved by God's grace plus this or that, regardless of whether this or that might be Law, rituals, works, endurance, abstinence. *We are saved by pure grace*, unmerited favor—not by works of righteousness (Titus 3:5). In Jesus we have life complete! (Col. 2:9,10).

CHRIST IS THE END OF THE LAW TO BELIEVERS

Verse 14: "Blotting out the handwriting of ordinances that was against us, which was contrary to us, and took it out of the way, nailing it to His cross."

What God demands, God provides: In Jesus, God was satisfied. In Matthew 5:17 Jesus said, "Think not that I am come to destroy the law, or the prophets: I am not come to destroy, but to fulfil." Romans 10:4 says, "Christ is the end of the law for righteousness to everyone that believeth."

It was God who consented to the death of Jesus; what Christ did, *God did by Christ*, willingly; both Father and Son were in agreement. Jesus willingly laid down His life for sin. He said, "Therefore doth my Father love me, because I lay down my life, that I might take it again. No man taketh it from me, but I lay it down of myself. I have power to lay it down, and I have power to take it again. This commandment have I received of my Father" (John 10:17,18).

God accepted the sacrifice of the blood of Jesus, and through His shed blood we have remission of sin—*minus ordinances*. The Greek verb used in verse 14 for "blotting" signifies "to plaster over." God's Law has not been destroyed, nor will it *ever* be. Jesus "plastered over" the Law of God. He did not destroy it—He *satisfied* God's Law.

Please notice that "the handwriting of ordinances"

which Jesus blotted out was AGAINST US. Great Bible scholars disagree as to what it was that was blotted out, but I firmly believe that Paul is here referring to the Law of Moses in its entirety. That Law presents a condemnation of the whole human race, "that all the world may become guilty before God." Writing to the believers at Ephesus he said: "Wherefore remember that ye being in time past Gentiles in the flesh, who are called Uncircumcision by that which is called the Circumcision in the flesh made by hands; *that at that time ye were without Christ, being aliens from the commonwealth of Israel, and strangers from the covenants of promise*, HAVING NO HOPE, AND WITHOUT GOD IN THE WORLD: But now in Christ Jesus ye who sometimes were far off are made nigh *by the blood of Christ*" (Eph. 2:11–13).

Jesus satisfied every jot and tittle of the Mosaic Law; therefore, since these ordinances are abolished, it is now the height of folly and vanity for believers to re-enact or to observe them, or to practice any part of them. Even though Bible scholars may not agree on what the ordinances were, *whatever* they were, they belong to an obsolete economy; the new economy has been in force ever since Jesus said, *"It is finished!"*

Notice that Paul uses the word "us" in verse 14, denoting both Jew and Gentile. In this dispensation of grace God does not distinguish between the Jews and Gentiles. He puts no stamp of approval upon circumcision nor disapproval upon *uncircumcision* as having to do with flesh. All of that ceased when Jesus finished redemption.

Writing to the Romans, Paul asked, "Do we then make void the law through faith? God forbid: Yea, we establish the law!" (Rom. 3:31). If the death of Christ was a divine imperative to cancel the indictment which the Law presented against man, then the death of Jesus does not destroy—but strengthens and completely ratifies the authority of that Law.

"By the law is the knowledge of sin." It follows that if the purpose of the Law was to confess the fact of man's sin—and man's exposure to the curse *because* of sin; and if the Law sets forth the mode of man's deliverance *from* it, then surely, since in Jesus the curse has been borne, the condemnation suffered and the sentence carried out, the Law of Moses has served its purpose and ceases to exist. What the Law of Moses taught in symbol is now enforced in reality. What the Law of Moses foreshadowed in type has now become a matter of history, and *Jesus is the end of the Law* for righteousness to everyone who believes. He, the one Mediator between God and men, now sits at the right hand of God the Father to make intercession for us, having by Himself, through His blood, purged our sins (Rom. 10:4; I Tim. 5:2; I John 2:1,2).

Not only has Jesus blotted out the handwriting, but He went further: "AND TOOK IT OUT OF THE WAY." What Paul is saying to the believers at Colosse is that the very document that declared judgment upon one and all has not only had the handwriting upon it blotted out, but *the very document itself*, even the very parchment upon which the handwriting was, has been TAKEN OUT OF THE WAY.

In the last part of verse 14 we are clearly instructed as to how Christ blotted out the handwriting, took away the very parchment, and satisfied God Almighty in all of His holiness and purity: by *"nailing it to His cross."* The idea Paul sets forth here is that when Christ was nailed to the cross, the condemning power of the Law was nailed there with Him.

"Now are we delivered from the law (that held us),

THAT BEING DEAD WHEREIN WE WERE HELD: that
we should serve in *newness of spirit*, and not in the oldness of the letter" (Rom. 7:6).

The divine truth here is this: When a sinner believes
on the Lord Jesus Christ, God exempts him from the divine sentence deserved because of his sin, this sentence
being canceled because of the sufferings of Jesus. The
guilt of the sinner was borne by the Man Christ Jesus
when He died on the cross. The guilt was laid on Him
by God—and when God laid on Jesus the guilt of all sinners and Jesus bore the sin of all the world, through this
method God took away the handwriting of ordinances that
was against us. *Jesus bore the sentence of that handwriting*; therefore God now remits (cancels) its penalty.
Jesus was despised and rejected of men; He was a man
of tears, heartbreaks and sorrows; He knew grief. He
bore *our* griefs and carried *our* sorrows; but Jesus the
spotless Lamb of God died *because He was "SMITTEN
OF GOD AND AFFLICTED"* (Isaiah 53:1—4).

Isaiah 53:6 is the only verse I have been able to
find in the entire Bible which begins and ends with the
same word: "ALL we like sheep have gone astray; we
have turned every one to his own way; and the Lord (Jehovah God) hath laid on Him (Jesus) the iniquity of us
ALL." (That takes in everyone and excludes no one.)
Jesus satisfied God concerning sin; *He bore the sins of
the whole wide world upon Himself* and nailed them to
His cross.

Verse 15: "And having spoiled principalities and
powers, He made a shew of them openly, triumphing over
them in it."

In blotting out "the handwriting of ordinances," God
at the very same time vanquished Satan—the old devil,
the deceiver and damner of souls. This verse plainly

refers to the wicked spiritual powers of the underworld. Paul speaks of the same wicked powers in Ephesians: "For we wrestle not against flesh and blood, but against principalities, against powers, against the rulers of darkness of this world, against spiritual wickedness in high places" (Eph. 6:12).

The devil has a kingdom; he is the head of untold millions of demons and wicked spirits. He is called "the god of this age" (II Cor. 4:4) and "the prince of this world" (John 16:11). He is not an "evil influence," nor is he "just an evil spirit."

Jesus met the devil in person—(Yes, there is a personal devil). The last of Matthew 3 and the first verses of Matthew 4 give the account of the baptism of Jesus, and immediately after His baptism He was led into the wilderness to be tempted of the devil. Satan met Him face to face and personally tempted Him through the avenues of the lust of the flesh, the lust of the eye, and the pride of life:

"And when (Jesus) had fasted forty days and forty nights, He was afterward an hungred. And when the tempter (Satan) came to Him, he said, *IF thou be the Son of God*, command that these stones be made bread." Jesus replied, "It is written, Man shall not live by bread alone, but by every word that proceedeth out of the mouth of God!"

The devil does not give up easily. He then took Jesus into the holy city Jerusalem, placed Him on a pinnacle of the temple and said to Him, *"IF thou be the Son of God*, cast thyself down: for it is written, He shall give His angels charge concerning thee: and in their hands they shall bear thee up, lest at any time thou dash thy foot against a stone." Jesus replied, "It is written again, Thou shalt not tempt the Lord thy God."

Satan then took Jesus "into an exceeding high mountain" and showed Him all the kingdoms of the world, "And saith unto Him, All these things will I give thee, if thou wilt fall down and worship me." Jesus then said to him, "Get thee hence, Satan! For it is written, Thou shalt worship the Lord thy God, and Him only shalt thou serve!" (Matt. 4:2–10). Then the devil left Him, and "angels came and ministered unto Him." Jesus conquered every temptation. He was tempted in all points as we are—yet was without sin.

"And having spoiled principalities and powers . . . ." Greek scholars tell us that the language here in the original tongue sets forth the idea of open warfare, with the victor conquering and spoiling—conquering, and then making the vanquished a spoil, as is done when a fallen foe is stripped of his armour. The figure is, that Christ stripped His spiritual foes of all power and authority.

The words "He made a shew of them openly" plainly portray a celebration after the battle. The spiritual foes which Jesus vanquished were exhibited after the victory and *angels came and ministered to the Victor!* All the spiritual world witnessed that battle and the exhibit which followed. Jesus utterly defeated the devil, triumphed over and conquered him; and now Jesus has in His possession the keys of death, hell and the grave.

Paul describes this victory in Hebrews 2:9,14–16:

"But we see Jesus, who was made a little lower than the angels for the suffering of death, crowned with glory and honour; that He by the grace of God should taste death for every man. . . . Forasmuch then as the children are partakers of flesh and blood, He also Himself likewise took part of the same; that through death He might destroy him that had the power of death, that is, the devil; and deliver them who through fear of death were all their lifetime subject to bondage. For verily He took not on Him the nature of angels; but He took on Him the seed of Abraham."

The devil is a defeated foe, a conquered enemy. He is still on the loose and "as a roaring lion walketh about, seeking whom he may devour"; but in the by-and-by Jesus will put him into the lake of fire and brimstone where he will be tormented forever and ever. He is defeated and he *knows* it; that is the reason he is working overtime today to damn every soul he possibly can. The battle between Jesus and the devil was not a hidden affair; it was done "openly." (Read John 7:4.) The battle was fought and Jesus won the victory openly, in the eyes of all.

Verse 15 closes with the words, ". . . . triumphing over them in it." In the cross of the Lord Jesus Christ, God the Father achieved victory over the ungodly powers of spiritual wickedness in high places (including the devil—the prince of all wicked powers). Through the death of His only begotten Son, God conquered him who had the power of death . . . that is, the devil.

On the cross Jesus purchased redemption, and the work of redemption was completed. Salvation was purchased and Satan was defeated. The blood of the Lamb of God wiped out the sentence passed upon all men. "The wages of sin is death," but the blood of Jesus Christ, God's Son, cleanses from *all sin*. In Jesus, through His blood, we have redemption and forgiveness of sins. Through the cross of Jesus, "the prince of this world is cast out."

To the believers in Colosse Paul says, "Do not let your minds be troubled concerning the teaching about the spirit-world, for all spirits are subject to Jesus, their divine Master. If the spirits are good, they are *His*

144

servants. (All good spirits are ministering spirits to the heirs of salvation.) If the spirits are evil they are conquered by Him, for He spoiled principalities and powers and conquered Satan with all of his emissaries!

Dearly beloved, I give to you the same advice Paul gave to the Colossians: *Do not seek to know things that are God's secret* (Deut. 29:29). What God wants us to know will be revealed to us by the Holy Ghost (I John 2:27; I Peter 2:6); and things having to do with the spirit-world, not revealed in the Word of God and taught to us by the Holy Ghost, should be left alone. We dare not step into the secret chambers of God's unrevealed truth concerning the spirit-world. Let me emphasize—*good* spirits, good angels, are servants of the most high God and the Lord Jesus Christ. *Evil* spirits are conquered and in subjection to His power! Leave the spirit-world alone and do not seek to know those things not clearly revealed in God's holy Word.

Verses 16 and 17: "Let no man therefore judge you in meat, or in drink, or in respect of an holyday, or of the new moon, or of the sabbath days: which are a shadow of things to come; but the body is of Christ."

I believe this verse has to do with eating and drinking as laid down in the Mosaic Law. While it is true that the Mosaic Law did not dwell as much on drinks as it did upon meats, it did include some rules and regulations about drinks and drinking vessels. Read Leviticus 7:20—27 and also the entire eleventh chapter of Leviticus. You will find that the people were forbidden to eat certain kinds of animals, fowl and seafoods, while others were declared fit for food.

On the eve of ministration, the priests were forbidden to use wine in any way. Also, certain kinds of vessels, if they had contained water that had been defiled, were

145

to be broken, while others were only to be washed and rinsed. Nazarites were to taste no product of wine.

The teachers of error in Colosse were demanding that the believers adhere to the dietetic injunctions of the Law of Moses; *but grace declares,* "FOR EVERY CREATURE OF GOD IS GOOD, AND NOTHING TO BE REFUSED, IF IT BE RECEIVED WITH THANKSGIVING" (I Tim. 4:4). The teachers of error forgot that Christianity rises far above such fleshly and physical restraints and distinctions. The new kingdom was "not meat and drink—but righteousness, and peace, and joy in the Holy Ghost."

No minister, regardless of his denomination, has any right to dictate to his parishioners the kind of food they are to eat nor the kind of clothes they are to wear, so long as they dress decently. If a believer wears clothes that hide the nakedness and do not cause sin through lust of the eye, no minister has any right to dictate what his congregation can and cannot wear. The Holy Ghost dwells within the bosom of every believer (Rom. 8:14), and will lead believers in matters of dress, as well as in what they should eat and drink.

It is a sin to eat anything that will destroy one's health, just as it is a sin to *drink* anything that destroys health. It is always gross sin to drink any kind of alcoholic beverages. We are commanded, "Look not on the wine when it is red, when it giveth his colour in the cup, when it moveth itself aright" (Prov. 23:31). "Wine is a mocker, strong drink is raging: and whosoever is deceived thereby is not wise" (Prov. 20:1). "WOE UNTO HIM THAT GIVETH HIS NEIGHBOUR DRINK, THAT PUTTEST THY BOTTLE TO HIM, AND MAKEST HIM DRUNKEN ALSO" (Hab. 2:15). These Scriptures clearly command total abstinence from alcoholic beverages.

Some religions teach that we are not to eat pork,

146

but there is no Scriptural command against eating pork in this day of grace. Personally, I do not eat pork, but I refrain for reasons of health and not for spiritual reasons. We should not eat anything that conflicts with the well-being of the body.

Still other religions teach that NO meat should be eaten on certain days, but all such teaching is man-made dogma; there is no Scriptural basis for it. Paul rebuked the Romans thus: "He that regardeth the day, regardeth it unto the Lord; and he that regardeth not the day, to the Lord he doth not regard it. He that eateth, eateth to the Lord, for he giveth God thanks; and he that eateth not, to the Lord he eateth not, and giveth God thanks" (Rom. 14:6).

Christianity knows no such thing as days, months or seasons. *Every* day is holy unto the Lord, and Christians should worship God every day. Ordinances of days, feasts, festivals and meats belong to an obsolete system—decayed and waxed old—having been nailed to the cross of our Christ. Christianity does not invite men to meet on certain days to feast and worship. (The church in the first chapters of Acts met daily, "to eat their bread with gladness and singleness of heart.") *Christianity is free*—it cannot be chained to "TIMES AND SEASONS." "Ye shall know the truth, and the truth shall make you free" (John 8:32). "If the Son shall make you free, *you shall be free indeed*" (John 8:36).

All of these ordinances were "a shadow of things to come." The original language suggests *a dim outline* of those substantial (eternal) blessings which are of Christ, and the Mosaic Law served a gracious purpose during the time it was in force; but now—"*Christ* is the end of the law for righteousness to everyone that believeth."

During the Dispensation of Law the temple was an

imperative; without the temple or tabernacle, Israel could not worship Jehovah. The temple with its apartments, vessels and furniture; the priesthood with its robes and priestly duties; the altar in the temple, the fire upon the altar, the cloud of smoke resting over the temple, the sacrifices of lambs, pigeons, doves, bullocks; the kind of offering and the special observances carried out in the temple; the ritual having to do with diet, dress, diseases—every minute detail of the Law was drawn up and given by divine authority to guide the Hebrews in their faith, worship and practices in daily life.

Remember—God called, ordained and commissioned Paul a minister to the Gentiles; and the Holy Ghost, speaking through Paul, declared that meat, drink, holy days, new moons and sabbath days "are a shadow of things to come." *The shadow is the intended likeness of the substance.* Almighty God did not fashion Christianity to resemble Judaism, but rather fashioned Judaism to resemble Christianity. The reality is not constructed to bear the likeness of the type, but the type is constructed to bear the likeness of the reality. The Mosaic economy was a *type* of Christianity and pointed to the future *existence* of Christianity. Every sin-offering in the Mosaic economy pointed to the Lamb of God who would be slain "in the fulness of time." All Israel looked for their deliverer. The Mosaic Law, with its blood offerings, pointed to the day when the divine sacrifice for sins would be offered, and the sacrifice under the Law testified to the death of the One who would come to settle the sin-question and purchase redemption. The blood offering under Law not only was a type of the blood to be shed—but it *guaranteed* that the blood *would be shed.*

A shadow is nothing in itself; it is empty and baseless. The Hebrew ceremonies could not give deliverance, nor could the blood of bulls, pigeons and lambs purge

148

the sinner "as pertaining to the flesh." The shadow had no power to purge the conscience, nor could it bring peace to the heart and assurance to the soul. The blood of a lamb could not satisfy Jehovah God; but in the fullness of time the *Lamb of God* came and offered HIS blood willingly. He, *the great High Priest of God*, willingly came, clothed in humanity. He took a body—and in that body He conquered and accomplished what the Law could NOT accomplish because of the weakness of the flesh (Rom. 8:1–3). The Law is no longer engraved on tables of stone; it is now written indelibly on "the fleshly tables of the heart." *Christ in you* is the fulfillment of God's holy Law in you because Jesus fulfilled every jot and every tittle of that Law (Matt. 5:18). *Every born again believer is now a royal priest* (I Pet. 2:9).

Paul is therefore asking, "Why return to the weak and beggarly elements? Christ has come; why return to the ritual—an obsolete religion of externals pertaining to meat, drink, garments, days—when you have received Christianity, and Christ (the completeness of God) dwells in you?"

Believers do not belong to a system—they belong to a body . . . the body of Christ. Read carefully I Corinthians 12:12–27. Paul clearly sets forth the fundamental truth that Jesus is the head of the Church, and that every born again believer, regardless of nationality or whatsoever, is baptized into the one body of which Christ is the head. Therefore we do not belong to an organization—we are part of an *organism* . . . the living body of Jesus Christ. In Colossians 3:3 we read: "For ye are dead, and your life is hid with Christ in God."

PAUL WARNS AGAINST FALSE MYSTICISM

Verse 18: "Let no man beguile you of your reward in a voluntary humility and worshipping of angels, intruding into those things which he hath not seen, vainly puffed up by his fleshly mind."

According to historians, the teachers of error in Colosse were called "Gnostics." They professed to be men of extreme knowledge . . . learned men, puffed up in their minds. They did not teach that Jesus was God in flesh, but that He was of the highest order of spirits, thus robbing Him of His divinity. They also exalted certain angels and gave them a part in man's salvation. They did not teach pure grace and fullness in Christ, but supplemented Jesus with angels and spirits.

Paul warned against such teachers and the warning holds good for us today. You and I need to be very careful; we need to "try the spirits and see if they be of God" (I John 4:1–4; II John 7–11). Paul warns the Colossians that these false teachers advertise an artificial humility and by means of that humility they will attempt to entangle the believers whom the Lord has set free. It is strange, yet true, that most false religionists are very humble in appearance and manner. They are kind, and many times go out of their way to demonstrate that kindness and false humility.

True spiritual humbleness is a gift provided only in the grace of our God. It is glorious to be persecuted for righteousness' sake, but there is no glory in being persecuted because of inexcusable ignorance! There are those who would wear rags and go barefooted in order to demonstrate their poverty and humility; they glory in a feeling of self-annihilation, as though they have forsaken all—when in reality they have forsaken nothing, because they have their reward: *They are doing what they do to the glory of the flesh.* In the words of Paul, they are "vainly puffed up by a fleshly mind." Some religionists are *proud* of their humility!

Never forget: The devil can be as a roaring lion—

150

or he can come as "an angel of light" or dressed in "sheep's clothing." He can come in many forms to deceive; he can take upon himself any form he desires in his attempts to lead the children of God astray or damn the unbeliever!

Bible history and antiquity clearly bear out the fact that the practice of spirit-worship and worship of angels was prominent during the first century of Christianity. It is a historical fact that at one time the archangel Gabriel was worshipped at Colosse. The statement "intruding into those things which he hath not seen" no doubt refers to visions which these false teachers professed to have had, although in reality they were liars using this scheme to lead astray those whose eye of faith was trained upon the Lord Jesus. Their teaching not only went beyond the Word of God, but beyond reason as well, "intruding into that which he hath not seen."

I believe most true ministers of the Gospel will agree with me that the hardest thing we face in the ministry is to get men to *accept the naked Word of God* by faith, without signs and wonders, thrills and chills. It is difficult indeed to persuade mankind to just simply believe God *because God is God*, and because God has spoken.

Faith does not ask "Why?" Faith does not ask to see; faith does not ask to feel. Christianity is the result of faith in the finished work of Jesus, the Son of God's love. We are *saved by God's grace* through faith, the just shall *live* by faith, and whatsoever is NOT of faith is sin! "For (whosoever) is born of God overcometh the world: and this is the victory that overcometh the world, EVEN OUR FAITH" (I John 5:4).

So then, *"faith cometh by hearing, and hearing by the Word of God"* (Rom. 10:17). These errorists in

Colosse refused to teach and preach simply *Jesus*—the head of the Church composed of blood-washed, born again believers . . . Jews, Gentiles, bond or free. They supplemented Jesus with their own teachings which were born in a mind "puffed up" by the flesh and dominated by spirits of darkness. They were too proud to learn— yet they affected a humility that was vile hypocrisy.

Verse 19: "And not holding the Head, from which all the body by joints and bands having nourishment ministered, and knit together, increaseth with the increase of God."

In this verse Paul definitely declares that Jesus is the head of all things. He is the beginning of the creation of God—"by Him were all things created." He is the head of the Church and the Saviour of the body (Eph. 5:21–33; I Cor. 3:11–15; I Cor. 12:12–27). The first part of this verse refers to Christ as head of His Church (Eph. 1:22 and Col. 1:18). The teachers of error did not hold to this fundamental doctrine, and the very fact of the gross error they taught was the result of their *rejecting Jesus* as very God in flesh and head of the New Testament Church.

Since they worshipped angels, they could not worship Jesus as Saviour and God, they could not adore His person. Since they insisted that believers be circumcised after the Law of Moses, they declared by the act of circumcision that God's grace is not sufficient for salvation and that Jesus did not tell the truth when He said, *"It is finished!"* If they taught the permanence of Mosaic ceremonies, they mistook the spirit and lost the benefit of the system which He had founded.

If the Mosaic ceremonies were to continue, they denied the finished work of Jesus; they denied that He had completed redemption's plan—and such teaching is spiritually fatal. "There is a way that seemeth right unto a man, but the end thereof are the ways of death" (Prov. 16:25). So long as a minister holds to the cardinal truths of the Bible, minor misconceptions can be tolerated; but when any preacher denies the cardinal truths—the paramount truth being the incarnation of Jesus—then Christianity becomes just another worthless religion. Christianity is God's answer to man's sin. Christ is the head of Christianity, He is the head of the New Testament Church and He is the Saviour of the body.

In the original Greek, the second phrase in this verse would read, ". . . from whom the whole body, through joints and bands supplied and compacted, groweth the growth of God." The same truth is stated in Ephesians 4:11–16. In the Church we have apostles, prophets, evangelists, pastors and teachers . . . "for the perfecting of the saints, for the work of the ministry, for the edifying of the body of Christ," till all the body come in the unity of the faith and the knowledge of the Son of God. Again Paul refers to Christ as the head of the Church, "From whom the whole body fitly joined together and compacted by that which every joint supplieth, according to the effectual working in the measure of every part, maketh increase of the body unto the edifying of itself in love" (Eph. 4:16).

What Paul is saying to the believers in Colosse is simply this: "Christ is head of the Church; by Him all the members of the body are *brought together*, and by Him (the head of the body) all members are *kept* together. Every born again believer is connected to the HEAD, and unity of the body *with* its head is essential to its growth."

It is interesting that Paul first mentions the head—which, of course, is essential to life and growth—and then goes on to explain that all the body is, "by joints

153

and bands," nourished and kept together. Therefore, in Christ *we have life*, we have *connection with God*, through His blood *we enter boldly* into the very holy of holies, and *through His power* we are held together, "kept by the power of God" (I Peter 1:5).

I am so glad the blood of Jesus has cleansed—and cleanses—from all sin (I John 1:7). I have the blood applied, and I am so thankful that Christ is my Mediator (I Tim. 2:5). I am so thankful that I am not worshipping angels and that I am not praying to spirits nor trusting in that which I have not seen. I am trusting in Him TO WHOM ALL POWER IS GIVEN IN HEAVEN AND IN EARTH! I am a member of the New Testament Church of which Jesus is the head. All born again believers are members of that body, and when the body is full grown, when the Church is complete, it will be caught up into the clouds to meet the Lord Jesus in the air (I Thess. 4:13—18).

WARNING CONTINUED

Verses 20—23: "Wherefore if ye be dead with Christ from the rudiments of the world, why, as though living in the world, are ye subject to ordinances, (touch not; taste not; handle not; which all are to perish with the using;) after the commandments and doctrines of men? Which things have indeed a shew of wisdom in will worship, and humility, and neglecting of the body; not in any honour to the satisfying of the flesh."

In this verse Paul is saying to all believers, "Since you *died with Christ* from the rudiments of the world, you are separated from the rudiments of the world by the death of Christ, because Christ IS the end of the Law for righteousness to all who believe. He came not to destroy the Law but to fulfill it, and this He did *literally*. Since this is true, why should believers entertain

154

the thought of *returning* to the rudiments of the world? The believer is dead to the Law . . . dead to ordinances; why then return to these dead forms when *the reality* is ours in Christ?"

Paul illustrates this in Romans 7:2–4: The wife is bound to her husband as long as he lives, but if the husband be dead she is free to marry another. In Galatians 2:19 we are clearly told that believers are "dead to the law." Therefore, if we are believers, we have died with the Lord; we are crucified with Him, risen with Him, and all things having been made new we are to walk in newness of life—not in the oldness of the letter. The Colossian believers had nothing more to do with rudiments of the world, with ordinances and Law; *they were free in the Lord Jesus Christ.*

In the Colossian church were those who still practiced the Jewish rituals and ceremonies, while others went even beyond this, worshipping angels and spirits. However, the main error of the false teachers was the attempt to impose upon the believers the ceremonial yoke of the Mosaic system. They were also teaching the deadly doctrine of communication between man and the spirit-world, which doctrine today is known as "Spiritism."

Christians should not be subject to ordinances and the Mosaic system because true believers are dead to these things. *Christ fulfilled them*—we are dead with Christ and our lives are "hid with Christ in God." Paul is saying to the Colossians, "Why should you for one moment suffer these things to be imposed upon you, having received the Lord Jesus and knowing the divine command of God concerning sin and salvation? Since you have higher Authority concerning eternal matters, why should you return to the doctrines of men?"

He then points out such teachings as "touch not,

taste not, handle not," which were the watchwords of the false teachers in Colosse. Today we still have religions that are founded upon that same doctrine—completely negative. According to their teaching, you must "give up and let go" in order to *get* saved, and then "give up, let go, touch not and handle not" in order to *stay* saved. Such a doctrine demotes the Lord Jesus and limits the power of God.

Bible scholars do not fully agree as to what Paul meant here in verses 21 and 22, but I personally believe he is saying that meats and drinks perish with using; they perish or cease to exist because they are consumed for the support of natural life, which is the purpose for which they were created and intended when properly used.

Salvation is entirely of the Lord, while the things with which man has to do are perishable. All creation is cursed. Before sin came there was no killing nor bloodshed; Adam was a vegetarian and would have remained so had he not sinned. Meats are for the body, and our Lord Himself said, "Not that which *goeth into* the mouth defileth a man; but that which cometh out of the mouth, this defileth a man. . . . Those things which proceed out of the mouth come forth from the heart; and they defile the man" (Matt. 15:11 and 18).

Christianity and spirituality are not based on external ceremonies nor upon that which we eat or drink. The gross error in this teaching is the looking for holiness in outward things rather than in the inward things of the heart. Such error is common in the church today. Men seek to be righteous and holy by abstaining from meats, drinks, and habits of life; but holiness is born in the heart of the believer. Christ is our holiness, and He abides within if we are truly born again. Man looks on the outward appearance but God looks on the heart, and to make the outside of the vessel clean will not satisfy God. It is not what we put into our mouth that makes or takes away spirituality: *it is what we harbor in the heart.*

It is gross sin to make a glutton of oneself in eating or drinking; but the individual child of God is to be led by the Spirit—not dictated to or dominated by a preacher, whether it be pastor or evangelist. If pork destroys your body you should not *eat pork*; but if, insofar as you know and your doctor advises, pork is not detrimental to your health, then it is not a sin to eat pork or any other meat, on any day, seven days a week. Likewise, if coffee or tea is harmful to your health you should not drink them; but if they do not hurt you physically, then certainly it is no sin to drink these beverages. We should not eat to excess—we should be temperate in all things; but no minister has authority on the basis of the Word of God to dictate to his parishioners what they can eat, drink or wear, so long as they conduct themselves in a Christian manner.

Christianity is not a system of rules, regulations or ordinances. Christianity is *Christ in you*—and with Christ in you, you have liberty—because "if the Son shall make you free, you shall be free indeed!" To destroy the body is to commit suicide—and whether we do it gradually by overeating or suddenly by taking an overdose of sleeping pills, it is wrong to destroy the body God gave us and in which the Holy Spirit dwells. If you are a believer, your body is the temple of the Holy Ghost and you should be very careful how you treat it, dress it and care for it. "As many as are led by the Spirit of God, they are the sons of God." Pastors are not to be "lords over God's heritage" (I Peter 5:3). True pastors are God's undershepherds—and the shepherd *leads* the sheep, he does not drive them.

In verse 23 we read, "Which things have indeed a

shew of wisdom in will worship, and humility . . . ." On the surface it may look good for a professed follower of Jesus Christ to follow poverty in daily living—wear humble clothes and eat bread that is stale and which can be purchased for one-tenth the price of fresh bread; but dearly beloved, we are not to advocate and live lives of poverty simply for the praise of men. There is a vast difference between living sacrificial lives for Jesus and living lives of self-enforced poverty to be seen of men.

Such practice may be "a show of wisdom," it may look good on the surface—but such practice does not necessarily mean that we are living the life of a saint nor that we are spiritually minded, because *these things can be false.* There is such a thing as false humility and it is a sin to direct attention and praise to one's self because of the practices of life. All praise, honor and adoration should be directed to the head of the Church, the Lord Jesus Christ.

Verse 23 closes with, "And neglecting of the body (the Church, which is the body of Christ); not in any honour to the satisfying of the flesh."

There are more ways to satisfy the flesh than by feeding it. There are those who are "vainly puffed up by a fleshly mind." The devil is a shrewd fellow; if he cannot cause a believer to become liberal or modernistic, he tries other methods to destroy the Christian's testimony. There are various and sundry ways in which the devil can rob us of our reward, and it is almost beyond imagination what some people will do in order to be noticed—even in the field of religion! Men many times glory in being what their fellowman aspires to be, but does not have the nerve to attempt.

In closing chapter 2 let me state again: To practice man-made doctrines ("touch not, taste not, handle not") indeed seems to show wisdom, and on the surface seems to show a will to worship and denotes humility and surrender. However, if one is practicing "touch not, taste not, handle not" to please a minister, a church, a religion—or to please his own thinking—then that person is not glorifying God, but on the contrary is neglecting the body of Christ. That person is satisfying the flesh instead of satisfying God. Whether we eat or drink, or whatsoever we do—we are to do it heartily as unto the Lord and for His glory. Anything we do (or refrain from doing) to satisfy the flesh or bring honor to one's self, *is sin*. "To him that knoweth to do good, and doeth it not, to him it is sin" (James 4:17).

COLOSSIANS —— CHAPTER THREE

1. If ye then be risen with Christ, seek those things which are above, where Christ sitteth on the right hand of God.

2. Set your affection on things above, not on things on the earth.

3. For ye are dead, and your life is hid with Christ in God.

4. When Christ, who is our life, shall appear, then shall ye also appear with him in glory.

5. Mortify therefore your members which are upon the earth; fornication, uncleanness, inordinate affection, evil concupiscence, and covetousness, which is idolatry:

6. For which things' sake the wrath of God cometh on the children of disobedience:

7. In the which ye also walked some time, when ye lived in them.

8. But now ye also put off all these; anger, wrath, malice, blasphemy, filthy communication out of your mouth.

9. Lie not one to another, seeing that ye have put off the old man with his deeds;

10. And have put on the new man, which is renewed in knowledge after the image of him that created him:

11. Where there is neither Greek nor Jew, circumcision nor uncircumcision, Barbarian, Scythian, bond nor free: but Christ is all, and in all.

12. Put on therefore, as the elect of God, holy and beloved, bowels of mercies, kindness, humbleness of mind, meekness, longsuffering;

13. Forbearing one another, and forgiving one another, if any man have a quarrel against any: even as Christ forgave you, so also do ye.

14. And above all these things put on charity, which is the bond of perfectness.

15. And let the peace of God rule in your hearts, to the which also ye are called in one body; and be ye thankful.

16. Let the word of Christ dwell in you richly in all wisdom; teaching and admonishing one another in psalms and hymns and spiritual songs, singing with grace in your hearts to the Lord.

17. And whatsoever ye do in word or deed, do all in the name of the Lord Jesus, giving thanks to God and the Father by him.

18. Wives, submit yourselves unto your own husbands, as it is fit in the Lord.

19. Husbands, love your wives, and be not bitter against them.

20. Children, obey your parents in all things: for this is well pleasing unto the Lord.

21. Fathers, provoke not your children to anger, lest they be discouraged.

22. Servants, obey in all things your masters according to the flesh; not with eyeservice, as menpleasers; but in singleness of heart, fearing God:

23. And whatsoever ye do, do it heartily, as to the Lord, and not unto men;

24. Knowing that of the Lord ye shall receive the reward of the inheritance: for ye serve the Lord Christ.

25. But he that doeth wrong shall receive for the wrong which he hath done: and there is no respect of persons.

THE BELIEVER'S UNION WITH CHRIST— ON EARTH AND IN ETERNITY

Verse 1: "If ye then be risen with Christ, seek those things which are above, where Christ sitteth on the right hand of God."

Notice the first word in this verse—"IF." That is, IF we ARE risen with Christ, then it is natural that we should seek the things above, where Christ now sits at the right hand of God the Father. It is natural for a sinner to seek the lusts of the flesh; but if the sinner be dead to sin and raised (quickened) with Christ, the new life gives forth new desires. There is a new nature within—Peter calls it "divine nature"; and having been delivered from the deadness of sin, now possessing the life of God in Christ, we are to seek the things above.

Ephesians 2:1–10 gives a magnificent word-picture (1) of the sinner—his condition and position; (2) the reason the sinner is changed from deadness to life, and (3) the result of that change. In these verses Paul describes the unbeliever as being dead in trespasses and sins, walking according to the course of this world—

children of disobedience; and then, in spite of this despicable picture, the Holy Spirit says, "BUT GOD, WHO IS RICH IN MERCY, FOR HIS GREAT LOVE WHEREWITH HE LOVED US, *even when we were dead in sins*, hath quickened us together with Christ . . . and hath raised us up together, and made us sit together in heavenly places in Christ Jesus: THAT IN THE AGES TO COME HE MIGHT SHEW THE EXCEEDING RICHES OF HIS GRACE IN HIS KINDNESS TOWARD US THROUGH CHRIST JESUS!" (Eph. 2:4–7).

In Ephesians 4:32 we read that God saves us for Christ's sake—not for our sake, not for our comfort nor for our glory. God forgives our sins and gives us eternal life "FOR CHRIST'S SAKE." God raises the sinner, gives him new life in Christ, and permits him to sit in heavenly places in Christ Jesus, *"That in the ages to come He might shew the exceeding riches of His grace in His kindness toward us through Christ Jesus"* (Eph. 2:7).

In Christ, God provided saving grace. Because of God's great love, He permitted Jesus to taste death for every man . . . to purchase redemption for every man at the tremendous price of His own blood. When the unbeliever *believes on the Son*, God forgives the unbeliever for Christ's sake, and positionally the forgiven sinner is placed in Christ in God. Therefore, *now* we sit with Christ at the right hand of God the Father in the heavenlies. The born again child of God is just as sure for heaven as if he were already there because positionally he is *already* sitting with Jesus at the right hand of God the Father.

"God, who at sundry times and in divers manners spake in time past unto the fathers by the prophets, hath in these last days spoken unto us by His Son, whom He hath appointed heir of all things, by whom also He made the worlds; who, being the brightness of His glory, and

162

the express image of His person, and upholding all things by the word of His power, *when He had by Himself purged our sins, sat down at the right hand of the Majesty on high"* (Heb. 1:1–3).

According to Paul's letter to the church at Ephesus, his letter to the Hebrew Christians, and Colossians 3:1–3, we born again believers are in Christ in God NOW; and since we hold this glorious position, the least thing we can do in appreciation for God's love is to seek those things above . . . "set our affections on things above and not on things of earth." We are pilgrims and strangers here; this earth is not our home. Our citizenship is in heaven, our head (the Lord Jesus Christ) is in heaven; the foundation of the New Testament Church is in heaven. We are members of His body—bone of His bone and flesh of His flesh (Eph. 5:30). Since this is true, *positionally* we sit with Christ at the right hand of God in the heavenlies NOW!

The same truth is set forth in Matthew 6:20 and 33, in Galatians 4:26, and in Philippians 3:14–20. The first few verses of Hebrews 12 tell us that Jesus endured the cross, despising the shame, looking to the glory beyond the cross—the glory that was set before Him. The sentence of sin called for suffering and death; therefore, Jesus left glory and came to earth's sorrow to pay the sin-debt. He suffered and died. He did not enjoy the cross, but He *endured* it because He saw the glory on the other side; and today He sits at the right hand of God the Father, exalted as none else in heaven or in earth. Christ is the One Mediator between God and men (I Tim. 2:5).

Since we then are risen with Christ, since we sit with Christ in heavenly places, we should seek the things that are above—and to seek or desire anything else would certainly be inconsistent. A sheep eats grass

163

because it is a sheep; a hog eats husks because it is a hog. We do not expect a hog to eat grass nor a sheep to eat husks, because it is not their nature to do so. By like token, sinners do not crave the things of God. An unbeliever had rather be at a dance or a card game than to be at Bible study or prayer meeting. It is natural for the sinner to crave, lust for and go after the things of the world; but it is just as *unnatural* for a *believer* to *love* those things. True believers do not seek things of the world; when one becomes a born again child of God, love for the world passes away.

One who has been born again, raised from the deadness of sin to new life in Christ, shudders at the memory of the lust and sin from which he has been delivered. His past condition—with its sin and guilt, misery, degradation and woe—holds no attraction for him. Having been *raised up*, he must still keep *looking* up, and he must seek those things which are above—things that are pure and righteous.

It is reasonable that the believer seek those things which are above because when we are born again we are in Christ and Christ is in us. Christ is above; our union with Him automatically leads us to think on Him; and where our treasure is, there will our heart be also. Promise and hope center in Christ. Spiritual blessings come *from Him*; we seek spiritual blessings and claim spiritual promises *in Him*.

Verse 2 is a command: "Set your affection on things above, not on things on the earth."

The Holy Spirit does not suggest, "If you feel like it, if you think it best, or if it is convenient." The command is plain: *"Set your affection on things above, not on things on the earth."*

That does not mean that we are to forget the earth,

our loved ones and our friends. We are pilgrims—but we are not to despise the comforts we may enjoy while traveling life's journey. Neither are we to allow the comforts, joys and pleasures of this life to come between us and the Christ who is above us. "THINGS ON EARTH" are only subordinate and instrumental, while "things above" are supreme, final and eternal. We can use certain things on earth to make life more enjoyable, more pleasant and comfortable; but we should never become so attached to these things that they hinder us in obeying the call of the Spirit and doing the work of the Lord at any time, anywhere. Many precious servants of God have become so attached to things on earth as to lose their grip on things above.

We should cling very loosely to things on earth, for if we become attached to them we are unworthy to claim to be followers of the risen Christ. *"Things"* are beneath Him; He wants our love . . . *all of it.* We are to love Him with all of our heart, soul, mind and spirit; we are to present our bodies a living sacrifice, holy and acceptable unto Him, "WHICH IS OUR REASONABLE SERVICE."

Believers have treasures laid up in heaven; what could earth add to such a treasure? What can earth afford that would outshine heaven's treasure? What honor could earth bestow upon one who is already seated with Jesus at the right hand of God the Father? What pleasure could earth offer that would outweigh the pleasures that are to be found at His right hand? What power on earth could be compared to the power possessed by the true believer who possesses divine nature and who is indwelt by the Holy Spirit? What fame does the world have to offer one who is already a son of Jehovah God, an heir of God and joint heir with His Son Jesus Christ? But in spite of "so great and precious promise," believers too often allow things on earth to so occupy mind and heart that they forget to seek "things above." Too many church members are like poor Esau, whose mess of pottage prevailed over his birthright! There are many today who are selling their spiritual birthright for much less than one bowl of soup!

In Matthew 22 Jesus gives the parable of those who were invited to the marriage feast but refused the invitation and made light of it. One went to his farm, one went to his merchandise, others went to their homes and families. They sought things in earth—they were not concerned about things above. When a person allows his mind to be fully occupied with things that are above, things of earth will automatically take second place.

Verse 3 is tremendous. I shall never forget the day I discovered this verse: *"For ye are dead, and your life is hid with Christ in God!"* What a position! What assurance! What hope! Greek scholars tell us that the original language reads, *"For ye died."* Verse 1 in this chapter announces the resurrection of the believer in Christ. All born again ones are raised with Christ, and Paul here points back to the time when the true believer *died* with Christ. Chapter 2:20: "Wherefore if ye be dead with Christ from the rudiments of the world . . . ."

The Colossian believers had died and had been raised with Jesus; therefore they were neither to seek nor savor the things of earth. Since they had died with Christ, were buried with Christ and raised with Christ, their life was to be totally different from their former state. One great Bible scholar said, "We *live not* in the flesh, but we *dwell* in the flesh." The flesh is the house of the spirit and the soul, but *only the house*; we LIVE unto the Lord.

Paul said, "I am crucified with Christ, nevertheless

I live" (Gal. 2:20a). When true believers died to the rudiments of the world and to the Mosaic system, their death was but a birth into a new life. Paul further declares, "Your life is hid with Christ in God."

Verse 4: "When Christ, who is our life, shall appear, then shall ye also appear with Him in glory."

To sum up the tremendous truth of these first four verses in chapter 3: If we are truly born again, "risen with Christ," automatically we are to "set our affections on things above." This is true because Jesus died to the world and *we died with Him*; He was buried and *we were buried with Him*; He rose again and *we rose with Him*. And when we accept the finished work of Jesus, we accept His death, His burial and His resurrection. We confess with the mouth and believe in the heart that Jesus was God's Christ; and when we confess that Jesus was God's Christ, we confess that He completely satisfied God . . . He finished the work He came to do: He purchased redemption and fulfilled every jot and every tittle of the Law. He suffered and tasted death for every man; He conquered him who had the power of death, "that is, the devil." When we truly receive Jesus we accept everything that He accomplished and fulfilled on behalf of the sinner; therefore *we are dead, and our life is "hid with Christ in God."*

Since we are hid with Christ in God, when the body (the Church) is complete, Christ the Head will return with the body. "When Christ who is our life shall appear, we also shall appear with Him in glory"—there is no "hope-so, think-so, nor maybe-so" about it. The bodies of believers will be raised incorruptible, living believers will be changed in the twinkling of an eye, and together we will be caught up in the clouds to meet Jesus in the air (I Thess. 4:13—18; I Cor. 15:51—55). Colossians 3:1—4 gives assurance and hope that is past

167

description in man's language. It is glorious to know that we are risen with Christ, that we are alive in Christ, hidden with Christ in God—and when Christ comes we will come with Him in glory. The Bride (the New Testament Church) will sit with Jesus on the throne of David in Jerusalem and will reign with Him right here on this earth for one thousand glorious years of peace!

It will be a happy day for some believers when they stop trying to repair what God gave up in the Garden of Eden. God made no provision for Adam's flesh; He said, "Dust thou art, to dust shalt thou return"; but in Genesis 3:15 God definitely promised deliverance of the spirit. Jesus came the first time to redeem the spirit (the inner man); not to *change the flesh*. It is true that the flesh acts differently when Christ abides in the heart; but Jesus is not going to repair these bodies. He will give us a *new* body when He comes in the Rapture at the first resurrection; we will be raised *incorruptible*.

When Jesus comes in the first resurrection, *"Mortality shall be swallowed up of Life."* When He who is our life comes, He will "CHANGE OUR VILE BODIES AND FASHION THEM LIKE UNTO HIS OWN GLORIOUS BODY." John tells us, "It doth not yet appear what we shall be: but we know that, when He shall appear, *we shall be like Him; for we shall see Him as He is"* (I John 3:1–3). Personally, I have my faith, trust, hope and eternal expectation in Him in whom dwelleth all the fullness of the Godhead bodily—the One in whom all believers are complete, which is the head of all principality and power (Col. 2:9,10).

If you are trusting in ordinances, dogmas, traditions, doctrines of men; if you have your confidence in the flesh—God pity you, for you are sailing in a hopeless vessel that is sure to sink! But if you are in Christ by faith, risen with Him through the operation of God, trusting in Him, when Christ who is our life shall appear, then shall we also appear with Him in glory. "If God be for us, who can be against us?" (Rom. 8:31).

CHRISTIAN LIVING

Verse 5: "Mortify therefore your members which are upon the earth; fornication, uncleanness, inordinate affection, evil concupiscence, and covetousness, which is idolatry."

In this verse Paul points out certain sins which were prevalent in heathendom, and which the Colossians had practiced during their sinful days; but now, since they are made alive in Christ, these sins must be abandoned entirely.

The first word in this verse is "Mortify." Then follows the word "therefore," which points back to verses 1 through 4. In other words, Paul is saying, "BECAUSE you are risen with Christ, *because* you are dead and your life is hid with Christ in God, and because when Christ who is our life does appear 'then shall ye also appear with Him in glory,' all former sinful practices must be abandoned."

It stands to reason that if "ye have died with Christ" . . . if the heart (the seat of life) is dead, all the members once kept alive by the heart and moved in lustful living should die also. They should die, killed by lack of nourishment and exercise. Born again ones must not exercise these members in former practices of life. They must be rendered useless and paralyzed by refusing to feed and exercise them.

Similar language is found in Romans 8:13 and also in Galatians 5:24. God does for us what we cannot do for ourselves, but He expects us to do for ourselves those things that are possible. Since we are new creations in Christ, since we possess the divine nature of God in the Holy Ghost who leads us; we can crucify the flesh and the lust thereof by starving these members that make up "the old man."

The "old man" is to be understood in the same spirit and manner as the emphatic declaration of our Lord: "If thy right eye offend thee, pluck it out . . . if thy right arm offend thee, cut it off" (Matt. 5:29). The lust that uses and debases these members as its instruments, is to be extirpated. Paul intends that these Colossians who once practiced lust and evil are to be completely yielded to God; they are to present their members "as instruments of righteousness unto God." The eye, the ear, the foot, the hand are members belonging to this body of flesh, and are subject to the "old man."

Notice the statement in verse 5: "Your members which are upon the earth." We are earthly creatures, we live in a body of flesh—and we shall remain in this body of flesh until we go to be with the Lord in death or when He comes in the Rapture. This statement points back to verse 2: "Set your affection on things above, not on things on the earth." Our citizenship is in heaven, the new man feeds upon heavenly things, and the old man is therefore in constant conflict with the *new* man. The minute a person is born again, war is declared between the old man and the new. Every truly born again believer has two natures. This fact is clearly taught in God's Word and many Christians need to know the fundamental truth concerning the two natures.*

As stated earlier in this study, it will be a happy day in the lives of some believers when they give up the idea of repairing what God gave up in the Garden of Eden—that is, *the natural body*. To Adam God said, "To

*Order my book, *The Two Natures*. Send coin, and order from The Gospel Hour, Box 2024, Greenville, S. C.

dust thou shalt return." The members of this body belong to earth and will return to dust; the earth is the sphere of their existence and operation. Believers are *a new creation in Christ Jesus* and are therefore to mortify the members that would serve the things of this earth, because these members are against the higher life which is hid with Christ in God. They are "of the earth—*earthy*."

The very essence of the members of the old man is earthy. We are tempted through the flesh, the flesh is the *source* of temptation, and it is the flesh that enjoys unrighteousness and lust. Jesus said to Nicodemus, "That which is born of the flesh is flesh, and that which is born of the Spirit is spirit" (John 3:6).

Let me again point out that the grace of God that *saves* us also sets up a classroom in our hearts and *teaches* us . . . grace both saves and teaches. (Study carefully Titus 2:11—15.) The person who possesses life in Christ—life that has its spring of living water in heaven—seeks to love with all his heart the things that are above and refuses to stoop to gratify the lust of the flesh in things of this earth which are in total opposition to the new and spiritual life that abides within.

Paul would not be a popular minister today, because he believed in naming sin; and in this verse he names various forms of sensuality:

Fornication; uncleanness; inordinate affection; evil concupiscence; and covetousness, which is idolatry. You will find practically the same words in Ephesians 5:3, II Corinthians 12:21 and Galatians 5:19.

Lewdness and lust were (and sometimes still are) used in worship. Such practice constitutes *pagan* worship, regardless of whether it is carried on in remote jungle areas or in the big cities of America. There is an abundance of practice of lust in the name of religion,

171

and the original language in this Scripture suggests the state of mind that urges or excites one to practice lewdness and impurity.

What Paul is saying to the believers is simply this: "Since you are new creations in Christ Jesus, risen with Christ, you are no longer to be guilty of fornication or any similar act of lewdness. You are to crucify lewd and lustful thoughts, or any other emotions and practices that issue from lust and lewd indulgences. Your mind is to be renewed in the Holy Ghost—spirit, soul and body preserved blameless" (I Thess. 5:23).

One of the outstanding signs of the end is that conditions will be as in the days of Noah, as in the days of Sodom and Gomorrah. If you will study the practices of the peoples of earth during the days just before the flood and just before the utter destruction of Sodom and Gomorrah you will find that lust was the outstanding sin. The minds of the people were married to lewdness and they practiced unnameable sins. If you could read some of the reports of the F.B.I. and other law enforcement agencies today, you would be shocked beyond words to learn the practices of the peoples in many of our leading cities in America and, sad to say, in some of our schools. Surely we are living in the closing days of this age of grace.

Verse 5 closes with ". . . and covetousness, which is idolatry." We do not need to travel to the jungles of South America or Africa to find idolatry—there is much of it right here in America. Jesus said, "Where your treasure is, there will your heart be also." The desire on the part of an individual to have more, and yet more, is idolatry. What one craves, he worships; and to such a god there is given the first thought of the morning, the last wish of the evening, and the action of every waking hour. When one's mind is completely occupied in gaining "things," that person is guilty of gross idolatry. The admonition of Jesus to His child is, "Seek ye first the kingdom of God and His righteousness, and all these things shall be added unto you" (Matt. 6:33).

Dear reader, what is *your* last thought in the evening before retiring? What is *your* last wish and desire before closing your eyes in slumber? What is your *first* thought in the morning . . . the first desire of your heart when you awake? What predominates your thinking during the hours of the day? Your god is the thing that occupies your mind and thoughts, thus leading into the actions and practices of the day. If you spend your hours desiring, scheming, planning and working to acquire more and more material possessions, if your appetite for "things" is never satisfied, then dear friend, according to the Word of God, you are practicing idolatry . . . you are worshipping an idol.

If we are in the right relationship with God, our first desire in the morning should be to look up and thank Him for the rest of the night. When we sit down at the breakfast table we should bow our head and thank God for the good food placed before us. Throughout the day we should live in an attitude of prayer—Paul says, "Pray without ceasing" (I Thess. 5:19). Throughout the day we should look up and give thanks unto Him who is our life, who is the giver of every good and perfect gift. If we let "things" crowd Him out of our thinking and out of our living, then our god is whatever occupies our mind and claims our utmost attention, regardless of what that object may be.

Verse 6: "For which things' sake the wrath of God cometh on the children of disobedience."

This is a definite warning that those who practice such sins as are named in the preceding verse can expect the wrath of God to be poured out upon them. (Study carefully Romans 1:18 and following.) They who practice such vice and sin not only disobey the divine commandments of God—they also violate the laws of health and the natural laws of the body, thereby bringing upon themselves disease, physical handicaps—and finally—*death*. Those who *sow to the flesh* reap corruption; but those who *sow to the Spirit* reap life everlasting.

"The wages of sin is death." When lust has conceived it brings forth sin and when sin is full grown it brings forth death. Sin has always paid singular wages, and always will. No man has ever gotten away with disobeying the laws of God and practicing the lust of the flesh. Such habits of life bring the wrath of God upon anyone who indulges.

Verse 7: "In the which ye also walked some time, when ye lived in them."

Before the Colossians were created new in Christ Jesus, before they were risen with Christ, they walked in these same lusts—but Paul reminds them that that period is now over. The old life was buried with Christ, a new life has dawned, and their walk is now in a new sphere—one in which, through the leadership of the Holy Spirit, they are to copy the walk of the Lord Jesus and seek to please Him in their daily life. They once followed the lust of the flesh and lived in these sins, but now these things are behind them. They live a new life because they have been created new in Christ Jesus.

As unbelievers they enjoyed such indulgences; they received gratification by practicing lusts of the flesh. They were addicted to such habits and because of the satisfaction of the flesh they believed that these things brought life and happiness. But now they are no longer in the flesh but in the Spirit because of the miracle of being raised with Christ (Rom. 8:9; Col. 3:1).

Some church members cannot live right, cannot stay right, because they have never been CREATED right! They have never had a change of heart, they *have never been born again.* There is a vast difference between joining a church or undergoing the rite of baptism, and being born of the Spirit. When one is born of the Spirit, the Spirit leads him into paths of righteousness *"for Christ's sake."*

Verse 8: "But now ye also put off all these; anger, wrath, malice, blasphemy, filthy communication out of your mouth."

The original language reads, *"But now ye too have put off the whole."* The Colossians had experienced a radical change: The heart in which lodged all those ugly, degrading lusts had been removed and a new heart had been placed where the old heart once was. Therefore, since the seat of life had been completely changed and a new heart had been given them, they had "put off the whole" and were *completely new*—a complete transformation through the miracle of the new birth.

The mouth speaks what the heart manufactures. In the heart of the unbeliever lies the possibility of violent emotion that literally boils within, and finally (like a volcano) erupts and proceeds out of the mouth. You may rest assured that cursing and dirty language do not originate in the mouth, but *in the heart.* Any person who cannot refrain from blasphemy and foul language needs only one thing—the new birth. "By their fruits ye shall know them," and a blaspheming tongue is simply giving forth words manufactured in an unregenerate heart.

This verse goes beyond what we know as cursing, blasphemy, or obscene language; it has to do with foul or abusive language in general. Any language connected with anger is unchristian and should be put out of the mouth and heart. There are times when a truly born again person will become angry—it is possible, but it ought not to be. We should never "fly off the handle." A Christian can speak words in sixty seconds that will be regretted for the next sixty years if that believer should live that long! We should pray in the early morning that God will sanctify our tongue; in the words of the Psalmist we should pray, "Let the words of my mouth and the meditations of my heart be acceptable in thy sight, O Lord, my strength and my Redeemer."

Jesus expresses it in these words: "If any man have ears to hear, let him hear. And when He was entered into the house from the people, His disciples asked Him concerning the parable. And He saith unto them, Are ye so without understanding also? Do ye not perceive, that whatsoever thing from without entereth into the man, it cannot defile him; because it entereth not into his heart, but into the belly, and goeth out into the draught, purging all meats? And He said, That which cometh out of the man, that defileth the man. For from within, out of the heart of men, proceed evil thoughts, adulteries, fornications, murders, thefts, covetousness, wickedness, deceit, lasciviousness, an evil eye, blasphemy, pride, foolishness: All these evil things come from within, and defile the man" (Mark 7:16—23).

It is not meat and drink that damn us—it is an unregenerate, unbelieving heart. When the heart is created new in Christ Jesus . . . when the old man becomes the new man in Christ Jesus . . . then the lusts that originate in the seat of life (the heart) automatically drop off and should not be so much as named among born again people. When the heart is made right through the miracle of God's Spirit, then feet, hands, eyes, ears and tongue behave themselves, because the heart is the machine which manufactures the practices of life. Those who cannot help

176

cursing a little, flying off the handle, getting angry and saying things that destroy their fellowman, *need the miracle of the new birth!*

Verse 9: "Lie not one to another, seeing that ye have put off the old man with his deeds."

Paul passes from sins of malignity and lust to the sin of lying, for the Colossians were now the children of Him who said, "I am the Truth." Since we are members one of another we should not lie one to another. He who is the Truth abides within us, we are risen with Him, we are to walk in newness of life, and since we are members of the same body we certainly should not lie *to* one another nor *about* one another. We have "put off the old man with his deeds," and one of the outstanding practices of the "old man" is lying. (The devil is the father of lies.)

Believers are to lie no more. First, "Ye are dead"— and dead men do not lie. Second, "Your life is hid with Christ in God," and since we are hidden IN the Truth, WITH the Truth in God, we certainly should not practice lying. We are dead to him who is the father of lies and alive unto Him who said, "I am the Truth."

The term "old man" in verse 9 has to do with the nature we received from Adam, the father of all living, who is the source and seat of our original nature in the flesh. This nature is called the "old man" because it existed prior to the new nature . . . the "divine nature" (II Peter 1:4).

The truth set forth here is simply this: In the same manner that a person puts off old clothes and dresses completely in different garments, the born again believer puts off the old man and puts on the new. We put on new garments—yea, "the righteousness of God in Christ Jesus." God does not repair the sinner, He does not repair the sinner's heart; the change goes deeper than repairs: *If we are truly born again, we have put on Christ.*

When one denies himself and abstains from meats, drinks and lustful habits, such abstinence may retard or discourage evil practices outwardly, thus leading friends to believe that this one is becoming a better person; but salvation consists of more than just *becoming a better person*; salvation is *a new man within* (II Cor. 5:17).

Jesus gives a clear-cut illustration of this in Matthew 12:43—45: "When the unclean spirit is gone out of a man, he walketh in dry places, seeking rest, and findeth none. Then he saith, I will return into my house from whence I came out; and when he is come, he findeth it empty, swept, and garnished. Then goeth he, and taketh with himself seven other spirits more wicked than himself, and they enter in and dwell there: and the last state of that man is worse than the first. Even so shall it be also unto this wicked generation."

If you will study this passage carefully you will notice that the unclean spirit *left* the man—he was not driven out nor put out; he walked out of his own accord. He sought rest but could not find it, so he said, "I will return into my house from whence I came out." It was his house; he left it without being asked to leave . . . he willingly departed. Then he said, "I will return to my house." Please notice that this house vacated by the unclean spirit was never indwelt by the Holy Spirit— it was *empty*; and certainly the heart of a believer could never be referred to as being empty. This man simply reformed—and self-reformation is worthless. When the spirit went back to the house he found it empty, swept, and garnished. He entered—and with him took seven other spirits "more wicked than himself"—*and the last state of that man was worse than the first.* He reformed, but he was never regenerated; he swept and garnished

178

the house—but the Holy Ghost never occupied it.

Verse 10: "And have put on the new man, which is renewed in knowledge after the image of Him that created him."

In Matthew 12 the evil spirit departed—but the house remained empty. In the case of the Colossians, the "old man" was put off—but the NEW MAN *was put on*. One man is old (and belongs to the past); the new man is not a matter of yesterday nor of tomorrow—but is an experience to be enjoyed every moment of every day. The new man does not only have to do with time—at the present moment being a new creation; he also has to do with quality of character. The new man is *"after the image of Him that created him."*

". . . They that are in the flesh cannot please God. But ye are not in the flesh, but in the Spirit, if so be that the Spirit of God dwell in you. Now if any man have not the Spirit of Christ, he is none of His" (Rom. 8:9).

"Which things also we speak, not in the words which man's wisdom teacheth, but which the Holy Ghost teacheth; comparing spiritual things with spiritual. But the natural man receiveth not the things of the Spirit of God: for they are foolishness unto him: neither can he know them, because they are spiritually discerned" (I Cor. 2:13,14).

The natural man cannot accept the things of God because he is carnal and cannot comprehend spiritual truth. Therefore, the new man to which Paul refers corresponds in certain elements to that of very God. The new man is *renewed in knowledge* after the image of God. Those of us who are born again possess divine wisdom because *"Christ is made unto us wisdom"* (I Cor. 1:30).

"The new man, which is renewed in knowledge after the image of Him that created him" does not refer to man's *person* nor to his *physical existence*; the "new man" is the converted, regenerated spiritual nature—not the man himself, but the *inner man*—"that which is born of the Spirit" (John 3:6). When we believe on the Lord Jesus Christ and receive Him as our personal Saviour, God creates within us "the new man, which after God is created in righteousness and true holiness" (Eph. 4:24).

This new creation . . . this new man with a new nature, is not the product of self-development. The new man is of God, not of reformation achieved by the individual through strong convictions of his or her will; nor is the new man the product of a change of creed, belief in religion or opinions (which may be the result of personal examination and conviction, but could never produce the new creation in Christ Jesus).

According to the Genesis account of creation, God made man in His own image; but when Adam sinned he marred and scarred that image—just how drastically we do not know. Certainly man today bears the marks and scars of sin, but just as truly as Adam was created in the image of God and retained that image until he sinned, now the *new* (the inner) *man* is created in His image, and the special point of divine resemblance is "knowledge." The teachers of error in Colosse boasted of their knowledge and were proud of their philosophy (Col. 2:2); but Paul reminds the believers that the very *knowledge of God* is implanted within us in the new man which is created in us in righteousness and true holiness.

I am not by any means suggesting that we possess divine omniscience, but every true believer *does possess* the Holy Ghost, who is the source of our knowledge. No one has any right, therefore, to question the height or depth of our knowledge (if our mind is free from bias and puffed up knowledge), if we allow the Spirit to teach us (I Cor. 2:10). If we are willing to be taught of the

Spirit we can certainly know in part the deep things of God (I John 2:27). It is true that now we see through a glass, darkly; but then face to face: now we know in part; but then shall we know even as we are known (I Cor. 13:12). Certainly in this body we shall never attain divine omniscience, but when we see Jesus we will be like Him in every respect and will possess divine omniscience in our glorified state.

Genesis 1:26–27 tells us that man was created in the image and likeness of God, and while there is no explanation as to what is meant by "the image and likeness of God," we do know that man is the most noble of all God's creations on this earth. God's command concerning murder teaches that man should not kill his fellowman because "IN THE IMAGE OF GOD MADE HE MAN" (Gen. 9:6). Such a statement is not made about any animal. The life of animals God delivered into man's hands for food, and nowhere in the Scripture is the life of an animal spoken of in comparison to the sacredness of human life. In James 3:9 we are warned of the consequences of using the tongue to praise God with one breath—and in the next breath cursing man, ". . . *made after the similitude of God.*" Man is a rational creature; man is immortal; and unlike any other creation of Almighty God, man as God's representative on earth bears the image of the God who created him!

It is true that certain privileges which man originally possessed and enjoyed were forfeited after the fall. Ignorance and spiritual death characterize man under the curse of sin and the unbeliever is "alienated from THE LIFE OF GOD" (Eph. 4:18); but the born again *believer* possesses the divine nature of God. Before the curse, man was filled with wisdom, purity, life, happiness—and was clothed with or by God's holiness. Man lost these glorious divine possessions when he sinned. (Personally,

181

I believe Shekinah glory danced about the bodies of Adam and Eve before the fall.)

"The new man, which is renewed in knowledge after the image of Him that created him," is fuller, lovelier, richer, with much greater intelligence and knowledge, with much nobler aims in view and a much higher form of life than the first Adam could ever have found in Eden, because the first Adam was "of the earth, earthy." The second Adam (the Lord Jesus Christ), in a body of flesh, made possible for you and me a life that could never have been attained by Adam in the Garden of Eden even had he never eaten the forbidden fruit.

It can be said of all truly born again believers, "In God we live, and move, and have our being." God is an eternal Spirit: *In the beginning . . . GOD.* God had no beginning, He has no ending, and He has willed man to be like unto Himself. Created in the image of God, man is capable of communing with God, capable of fellowshipping with God, and in the final consummation of all things when time fades into eternity, in the Bride and all things created new God will have what He willed in the beginning: *Sons who will worship Him supremely, honor Him only, and serve Him* world without end! God is a jealous God, and from the beginning He has sought a people to love, honor and cherish . . . a people who would worship and serve only the true God.

Verse 11: "Where there is neither Greek nor Jew, circumcision nor uncircumcision, Barbarian, Scythian, bond nor free: but Christ is all, and in all."

In this verse, Paul points out that all distinctions having to do with race, religion, creed or background are forever wiped out in the new man. Notice the four pairs of people and religious ceremonies that bore definite distinctions before the day of grace:

1.   The *national distinction* between Greek (Gentile) and
     Jew.   The kingdom was presented first to the Jew,
but the Gospel is also to the Gentile in this day of grace
(Rom. 1:16).

2.   The second group has to do with *religious distinction*:
     "Circumcision and uncircumcision."   Circumcision
belonged to the Jewish world; it was the seal of the
covenant in the flesh.   Uncircumcision pertained to non-
Israel—that is, the world beyond the chosen seed who
were the elect of God concerning religious blessing.
Those of the uncircumcision were known as "Gentile
dogs."

3.   *"Barbarian and Scythian"* applied to the whole world
     beyond Israel, there being various distinctions in
that world itself.   According to Josephus and other historians, some of these people were refined people of
culture, while others were wretched and base beyond
description.   According to historians the Scythian is at
the lowest point of barbarianism—we might refer to him
as a savage or a bushman.   In Paul's day these people
were regarded as being at the bottom of the scale of
humanity.

4.   The terms "bond" and "free" represent a *social
     distinction* which was very common in those coun-
tries in the days of Paul, and which still exists in some
countries today.

     Paul points out that in spite of one's nationality or
religion; whether a person be civilized or savage; whether
he be bond or free, IN CHRIST *all people* become new
creations.   Regardless of former status, a believer is
risen with Christ, possesses divine nature and is led
by the Holy Ghost.   Regardless of the color of his skin,
the religion which he may have practiced, his background
from the standpoint of being savage or civilized, bond

or free, when a person believes on the Lord Jesus Christ as Saviour, that individual becomes one of us who belong to the body of Christ: "YE ARE ALL ONE IN CHRIST JESUS!"

Paul does not mean that a man loses his nationality when he becomes a Christian, nor does he mean that social rank is done away with in joining the church. The blood of a Jew does not become Gentile blood when the Jew is born again; the blood of a Gentile does not become that of a Jew when the Gentile is saved; but *both Jew and Gentile become members of the same body*, the same spiritual kingdom. The Barbarian may be rude and rough, but when he becomes a Christian his habits of life change. He does not, however, lose his nationality—he is still a member of the same human family from the standpoint of the flesh; but there is a new man IN the flesh—*the Lord Jesus Christ.*

Paul is pointing out to the Colossians the fact that the Gospel knows no racial barriers nor national limitations . . . it is not bound by geographical limits. The Greek is not nearer to Christ because of his philosophy and learning than is the savage with his lack of knowledge and education. The Gospel will soften the heart of the savage and save him just as the Gospel softens the heart of the Greek. Regardless of whether slave or free man, whether gypsy or polished citizen . . . regardless of race, creed, language, pursuit of life, color, climate, dwelling, social position or character—regardless of *anything* and *everything*—the Gospel of the marvelous grace of God comes with the invitation, *"Believe on the Lord Jesus Christ, and thou shalt be saved!"* "As many as received Him, to them gave He power to become the sons of God, even to them that believe on His name, which were born . . . born of God."

Paul taught the Colossians that in the Church of

the living God, the sphere of the new man's joy and spiritual blessing does not come as a result of his outstanding background, nor is it limited because of his degraded background. The slave can be just as happy in the Lord and live just as abundantly in Christ as can the Jew or the man of culture and renown. The slave and the free man unite their voices in the same song of praise to the Saviour. They drink from the same wells of living water, they commune in the same body—for we are all members of one body (I Cor. 12:12,13).

Paul was an educated man, yet he taught that education is not a necessity for one to be taught of God and to search for the deep things of God (I Cor. 2:10,11). It is not essential that civilization lay the groundwork before the Holy Spirit can work—the Holy Spirit can work in the heart of a heathen and make a new creation from the vilest of savages, for when the savage of the jungle hears the Gospel and receives the Lord Jesus Christ, he becomes a citizen of heaven—a member of the New Testament Church. The glorious fact of Christianity is that it knows no barriers, no limitations. Christianity is not divided into ranks or groups; we are all members of the same body, we have all been made to drink into the same Spirit, and we are all one in Christ.

Read and study John 4 and you will see a most beautiful picture of what Paul is teaching in this portion of Colossians. Jesus sat beside Jacob's well as a Gentile woman came to draw water. She was of despicable character—a woman of the streets who had had five husbands and was at that time living with a man who was not her husband. Yet Jesus saved her and this heartbreaking harlot became a soul-winning Christian. Because of her testimony many Samaritans were born again. Yet, when Jesus asked her for a drink she could not understand why a Jew would ask anything of a hated Samaritan. In

185

the course of the conversation, Jesus proved to this woman that God's love knows no racial barriers, no human limitations, and that God's wisdom knows all about us. God's love can reach the vilest of sinners. The Samaritan woman threw down her waterpots and ran to the city, witnessed to the men there and a great revival broke out.

I am so glad Jesus died for the scuttlebum, the harlot, the doper, the alcoholic. I am just as glad that He died for the college professor, the bank president, the lawyer, the doctor, the governor. We build missions on the street of forgotten men and women, but someone should get a vision and build a mission on the avenue of other men who are forgotten—cultured, "up-and-out" people of high social standing; civic leaders who from the monetary and educational standpoint have risen to the heights of earthly glory and yet have never embraced the blood-bought salvation of Calvary. They need Jesus just as badly as do those on the streets and back alleys of forgotten men, and Jesus loves that group just as much as He loves the gutter-drunk and the "down-and-out." The invitation is, *"Whosoever will*, let him drink of the water of life freely!"

Verse 12: "Put on therefore, as the elect of God, holy and beloved, bowels of mercies, kindness, humbleness of mind, meekness, longsuffering."

In verse 12 Paul points out certain graces that every true believer should demonstrate in daily living. Paul first specified the sins that mark the old man—sins manufactured by the old nature; and now he points out virtues which are connected with and are the fruit of the new creation within. He is saying in this verse, "You have put on the new man, you are risen with Christ; therefore, enjoy the all-sufficiency of Christ and demonstrate these elements of Christian character."

186

Paul said the same thing to the Galatians, in essence: "But the fruit of the Spirit is love, joy, peace, longsuffering, gentleness, goodness, faith, meekness, temperance: against such there is no law. And they that are Christ's have crucified the flesh with the affections and lusts. If we live in the Spirit, let us also walk in the Spirit. Let us not be desirous of vain glory, provoking one another, envying one another" (Gal. 5:22—26).

The believer is to demonstrate by his actions the possession of the new man. Christians are to be obliging, generous, tender, humble, kind, forgiving, longsuffering, meek and temperate in all things. Christians are not to desire vain glory; believers should never be puffed up. What do we have to be puffed up *about*? If we had justice we would be in hell! We are the recipients of God's mercy and we should be humble and thankful that God so loved us as to permit Jesus to take our place on the cross and suffer and die in our stead.

These graces should be put on and displayed by "the elect of God, holy and beloved." Every believer belongs to the family of God. The Church as a body was elected before the foundation of the world, and every true believer is predestined to be conformed to the image of God's Son; however, individuals become members of that body by receiving the Lord Jesus Christ (John 1:12,13).

The body, the *New Testament Church* of which Jesus is the head, was *elected*; but *individuals* either *receive* or *reject* the Lord Jesus. John 3:18 tells us in simple, plain, understandable language who is saved, who will go to heaven; who is lost and who will burn in hell. That same verse clearly points out WHY people are saved and enter heaven, and why people are *unsaved* and go to hell. Read it, study it, analyze it, believe it. Those of us who are believers belong to the elect of God, the body of Christ; and in Christ we are holy, spotless,

187

blameless; in Christ we are beloved. God saved us for Christ's sake. God's love is extended to us only upon the merit of the shed blood of His only begotten Son.

Verse 13: "Forbearing one another and forgiving one another, if any man have a quarrel against any: even as Christ forgave you, so also do ye."

Not only is the believer to be humble, meek, long-suffering and gentle, but the believer is also to manifest mercy and goodness in forgiving. There will be offences; Jesus said, "In the world ye shall have tribulation: but be of good cheer: I have overcome the world" (John 16: 33). There may even be just ground for offence, but we are never to permit resentment or retaliation. It is very difficult to love some people; but those whom we find impossible to love, Christ will love *through us* if we will only let Him. As believers we should demonstrate the spirit of God's love as set forth in Ephesians 4:32. God for Christ's sake forgave us, and Paul says we are to forgive one another, *"even as God for Christ's sake hath forgiven you."*

We as believers are to forgive one another because Christ has forgiven us. We are to forgive fully and freely, and we are to forgive at once . . . we are not to hold malice nor bear a grudge. We are to forgive now and forever—NOT *seven* times, but in the words of Jesus, *"seventy times seven!"* As believers and followers of the Lord Jesus we should be strong enough and big enough to forgive, without demanding apology on the part of those who have offended us. It may be painful, it may take an extra portion of grace—but Christians should forgive and forget, remembering that God has forgiven us for the sake of His precious Son. Not only has God forgiven us, but He cast our sins into the depth of the sea; He put them behind His back, to be remembered against us no more. When the sinner believes on the Lord Jesus

Christ and trusts Him as personal Saviour, God blots out every transgression, forgets every sin that person has ever committed and justifies him on the merits of the finished work and the shed blood of the Lord Jesus Christ.

Verse 14: "And above all these things put on charity (love), which is the bond of perfectness."

In this verse Paul calls love "the BOND of perfection"—NOT "perfection." "Bond of perfection" means that which holds together all the graces which constitute perfection. *Perfection* consists of many, many graces—each grace in its own place and relationship to spiritual perfection, each grace in its own circle and sphere, but ALL held together by love!

"Though I speak with the tongues of men and of angels, and have not love, I am become as sounding brass, or a tinkling cymbal. And though I have the gift of prophecy, and understand all mysteries, and all knowledge; and though I have all faith, so that I could remove mountains, and have not love, I am nothing. And though I bestow all my goods to feed the poor, and though I give my body to be burned, and have not love, it profiteth me nothing. . . . And now abideth faith, hope, love, these three; but the greatest of these is love" (I Cor. 13:1–3, 13).

Love is the highest element of divine perfection: "God is love" (I John 4:8). Love creates perfection, but in this verse it is represented as the *bond* which sustains and supports spiritual perfection. No grace is complete without love. Without the love of God, knowledge is worthless. Knowledge without the love and the fear of God is selfish and leads only to human pride and vanity of mind. *Love* is UNselfish. *God* so loved that He willingly gave His only begotten Son. *Jesus the Son* so loved that He willingly laid His life down, that sinners might be saved through faith in His finished work (John 3:16; John 10:18). Sin is selfish in all forms and varieties. Such selfishness must be conquered and put down before the love of God can have right-of-way in the heart. Jesus said, "Love the Lord thy God with all thy heart, and with all thy soul, and with all thy mind . . . and . . . love thy neighbor as thyself. On these two commandments hang all the law and the prophets" (Matt. 22:37–40).

The greatest need in the true church today is an old-fashioned revival that will literally baptize believers in, and fill them with, the love of God. When we love God as we should, we will love the brethren and will have a deep concern for those who are not brethren and who are out of the ark of safety. May God send us a revival that will rekindle the fires of His love in the hearts and lives of born again believers!

Verse 15: "And let the peace of God rule in your hearts, to the which also ye are called in one body; and be ye thankful."

This verse continues Paul's exhortation to the believers in the Colossian church, admonishing them to allow the peace of Christ to rule and reign in their hearts. The "peace" of which Paul speaks here goes much deeper than just peace among brethren and harmony in the local assembly. With Paul, *peace is synonymous with happiness.* Peace denotes a calm mind and a yielded spirit not easily upset or disturbed by adversity; a heart, mind and spirit not overshadowed or darkened by sin and a guilty conscience. Paul is speaking of the peace that removes the fear of death and dread of meeting God: "Thou wilt keep him *in perfect peace* whose *mind* is *stayed on (Jesus)*" (Isaiah 26:3).

Certainly nothing would destroy such peace more quickly than for a believer to indulge in those foul, despicable passions against which Paul warns all believers in verses 5 through 9. By the same token, there is nothing so conducive to purity and the permanence of peace as for the believer to cultivate the graces named in verses 12, 13 and 14. Paul is simply saying, "You have dropped the angry passions and vices that are the fruits of unbelief and have put on the graces and virtues which the love of God provides. Therefore, the peace of Christ shall reign within you; and *since* the peace of Christ reigns within you, His peace produces happiness that will be expressed in psalms, hymns and spiritual songs."

Jesus said, "Peace I leave with you, my peace I give unto you: Not as the world giveth, give I unto you. Let not your heart be troubled, neither let it be afraid" (John 14:27).

The Lord Jesus Christ, the Son of God's love, purchased this peace with His precious blood, and His peace is the result of true faith in His blood, shed for the remission of sin. Believers are not just to *possess* this peace, but they are to allow the peace of God to *rule in their hearts* in undisputed and uninterrupted supremacy. Christ's peace is to be in complete control, absolute ruler in the heart of the Christian.

Paul is simply saying, "Let peace govern your heart and life—and happiness will be the automatic result. Every fear and every doubt will disappear." Paul desired that his children in the Lord enjoy their spiritual birthright. He wanted their souls to enjoy unbroken peace—the peace that comes only by and through the gift of God—the shed blood of His only begotten Son, the Lord Jesus.

The peace Paul speaks of here is *God's gift*—man cannot cultivate nor produce this peace by good living or by good works. All believers are called to this peace:

191

"To the which also *ye are called in one body.*" (Read I Cor. 12:12–15 and Eph. 5:25–30.) The Gospel of the marvelous grace of God invites man—not to a life of misery nor a life of "don'ts"—but to a life of happiness, abundance, pleasures forever more and *peace* (John 14:27; Isaiah 26:3) that surpasses all understanding. The grace of God does not bring internal discord, but rather a heart that is filled and possessed by the peace of God (Rom. 5:1; Col. 3:15), and all believers are called to the possession of this peace.

Verse 15 closes with the command, *"Be ye thankful."* Certainly any person can be happy and thankful when all goes well and when everyone speaks well of him; but the Christian is to "give thanks in ALL things." The only person who can smile through a veil of tears and praise God in the midst of tragedy is a born again, Spirit-filled, fully surrendered child of God!

One of the outstanding marks of consecration and spirituality is thankfulness. God pity the believer who grumbles and finds fault when he knows that God gives him the very air he breathes and the sunshine that is a necessity of life. Every good gift and every perfect gift comes from God, who has bestowed upon us every thing good and every thing worthwhile. Jesus loved us so much that He was willing to die for us, and since we know Him as our personal Saviour and are called to this wonderful peace that surpasses all understanding, we certainly should be thankful to our great God who loved us and proved His love by giving the best Heaven had. It is a sin to be unthankful.

If we are born again we know that nothing can happen to us without God's permission, and *whatever* happens to us is for our good and God's glory. Romans 8:28 is just as true as is John 3:16; so, fellow believer, count your many blessings, name them one by one—and it will surprise you what the Lord has done! *"And be ye thank-ful."*

Verse 16: "Let the word of Christ dwell in you richly in all wisdom; teaching and admonishing one another in psalms and hymns and spiritual songs, singing with grace in your hearts to the Lord."

Jesus said in John 6:53, "Except ye eat the flesh of the Son of man, and drink His blood, ye have no life in you." What He was saying is simply this: "Unless you accept my word literally, literally appropriate it into your heart and take it into the inner man, you have no life; because it is the *Word* that *brings* life!" Peter explained: "Being born again, not of corruptible seed, but of incorruptible, *by the Word of God*, which liveth and abideth for ever" (I Peter 1:23).

Jesus said, "Verily, verily, I say unto you, He that heareth my word, and believeth on Him that sent me, hath everlasting life, and shall not come into condemnation; but is passed from death unto life" (John 5:24). Ephesians 2:8 tells us, "By grace are ye saved through faith, and that not of yourselves; it is the gift of God." Romans 10:17 says, "So then faith cometh by hearing, and hearing by the Word of God." To the Corinthians Paul wrote, "I have begotten you through the Gospel" (I Cor. 4:15b). The life of a believer *begins* when the *unbeliever* hears the Word, believes the Word, and receives the Word into his heart (Rom. 10:13–15).

Peter said, "As newborn babes, desire the sincere milk of the Word, that ye may grow thereby" (I Peter 2:1,2). Paul told young Timothy, "Study to shew thyself approved unto God, a workman that needeth not to be ashamed, rightly dividing the word of truth" (II Tim. 2:15).

Apart from the Word of God there is no spiritual life

193

nor spiritual growth; apart from the Word of God it is impossible to fulfill the duties of a believer. That is why Paul said to the Colossians, *"Let the word of Christ dwell in you richly in all wisdom."*

What is the Word? "In the beginning was the Word, and the Word was with God, and the Word was God. The same was in the beginning with God . . . and the Word was made flesh, and dwelt among us, (and we beheld His glory, the glory as of the only begotten of the Father,) full of grace and truth" (John 1:1,2,14).

The Word of God is actually Jesus, for Jesus was God in the flesh (II Cor. 5:19). He was the Word wrapped up in flesh and brought down to man; He saved those who heard Him and received Him; and today He saves those who hear Him through the Word and exercise faith brought BY the Word. Faith in the finished work of Christ and in His shed blood brings salvation through the grace of God.

This may be surprising to some—but listen: "He that rejecteth me, AND RECEIVETH NOT MY WORDS, hath one that judgeth him: THE WORD THAT I HAVE SPOKEN, THE SAME SHALL JUDGE HIM IN THE LAST DAY" (John 12:48). We will never know this side of eternity the importance of God's holy Word. No wonder the devil is trying so hard today to destroy the Word of God!

". . . In all wisdom . . . ." There is only one place to obtain the right kind of wisdom: "The fear of the Lord is the *beginning* of knowledge" (Prov. 1:7), and "If any man lack wisdom, *let him ask of God*, who giveth to all men liberally" (James 1:5). Paul tells us in I Corinthians 1:26–31, "For ye see your calling, brethren, how that not many wise men after the flesh, not many mighty, not many noble, are called: But God hath chosen the foolish things of the world to confound the wise; and God hath chosen the weak things of the world to confound the things which are mighty; and base things of the world, and things which are despised, hath God chosen, yea, and things which are not, to bring to nought things that are, THAT NO FLESH SHOULD GLORY IN HIS PRESENCE. But of Him are ye IN CHRIST JESUS, WHO OF GOD IS MADE UNTO US WISDOM . . . and righteousness, and sanctification, and redemption, that, according as it is written, HE THAT GLORIETH, LET HIM GLORY IN THE LORD."

America needs men today who will stand behind the sacred desk, open God's holy Bible, and preach the Word of God as it is laid down, looking to the Holy Spirit as their teacher, studying diligently and faithfully, to show themselves *approved unto God*—not unto their denomination nor people in the pew. Paul said to young Timothy, "Preach the Word, be instant in season, out of season, reproving, rebuking, exhorting, with all longsuffering and doctrine" (II Tim. 4:1–3).

". . . Teaching and admonishing one another in psalms and hymns and spiritual songs, singing with grace in your hearts to the Lord." No person can teach, preach, or instruct another in the things of God unless he is himself literally saturated with the Word of God. America needs ministers who are saturated with the Word of God rather than with teaching from denominational seminaries or doctrines set forth by men.

The members of a church with such a pastor *will* admonish one another, singing psalms, hymns and spiritual songs, making melody in their hearts to the Lord. The devil cares not how long, how sincerely nor how fervently a minister may preach, so long as he does not preach the pure, unadulterated Gospel of the marvelous grace of God. The devil can handle any message not saturated with Scripture. Read Peter's sermon on the day of Pentecost and you will find it to be Scripture— or *the essence of Scripture*—from beginning to end; and at its close three thousand souls were saved! Peter had more souls saved in five minutes of pure Gospel preaching than most of us have in a lifetime. God help us to preach the Word without fear, favor or apology, for it is "the power of God unto salvation to everyone that believeth." It is the seed that brings new birth; it is the bread of life; it is the water of life; it is the light of life. We are begotten by the Gospel, and we will be judged by the Word of God.

Verse 17: "And whatsoever ye do in word or deed, do all in the name of the Lord Jesus, giving thanks to God and the Father by Him."

In verse 16 Paul speaks of the *meeting* of the church, pointing to the house of God when he mentions admonishing one another in songs, hymns and spiritual songs, with grace in the heart to the Lord; but verse 17 goes further than that: Whatever the believer does in word or in deed, *all* that he does or says should be in the name of the Lord Jesus. All speech, all action, every detail of daily living and practice is to be done in the name of the Lord.

What does it mean to do whatsoever we do in the name of the Lord? It means simply this: When we speak in His name or commit an act in His name, we speak and act under His leadership—under the direction and the sanction of the Holy Spirit—with deep conviction that what we are doing or saying meets with His approval. The highest form of Christian dedication is when, with a sincere heart, we recognize Christ in everything we say or do—not just in the church or in a religious service, but in our business life, in our daily living, in our recreation—*whatsoever* we say or do.

It is not difficult for believers to do all they do in the church or in religious services in the name of the Lord; but it is another matter when, outside the church, we are dealing with friends and neighbors in everyday life. When our every thought, motive, action, speech, and all details of our daily life are carried out in the name of the Lord and to His glory, being fully persuaded that He is leading and sanctioning everything we do or say, such is the height of spiritual dedication and Christian consecration.

Paul is not suggesting that when we go to the grocery store to purchase a loaf of bread, we should say to the groceryman, "I am buying this bread in the name of Jesus to the glory of God." No, that is not the idea at all. We should be very careful that our good is not evil spoken of, and realize the difference between full surrender, complete dedication—and self-righteousness. God deliver us from becoming "holier than thou" or self-righteous.

Verse 17 closes with the words, "giving thanks to God and the Father by Him." All true thanksgiving to God the Father is directed through Christ the Son; and as we give thanks to God by Christ, in the same manner we should *think* all things, *speak* all things and *do* all things in Christ's name. He is the Mediator between God and man (I Tim. 2:5). All blessings come through Him, and through Him the believer should direct all thanks to God the Father. It was God who "so loved the world" that He permitted Calvary.

Every believer should memorize Romans 5:11. After naming the seven-fold fruit of *justification by faith* in the finished work of Jesus, Paul says, "And not only so, BUT WE ALSO JOY IN GOD through our Lord Jesus

197

Christ, by whom we have now received the atonement." Always thank God that He permitted Jesus to make the atonement possible. Never forget that had it not been for the grace of God the Father (Heb. 2:9), had it not been for the *love of God*, there would never have been a Man named Jesus.

Verse 18: "Wives, submit yourselves unto your own husbands, as it is fit in the Lord."

The submission Paul mentions here is of a different source and form from the forced subjection of slavery found in heathen lands. The wife of a believer is admonished to *willingly* submit to her husband. If God has joined man and woman together, if the union is a result of pure love, the submission of the wife to the husband is prompted by a wife's affection and the natural tendency to lean on the husband for support. The wife was created by God to be the "helpmeet" of man. The very word "helpmeet" suggests that the wife is to be auxiliary and not the principal one in the household.

Writing to the believers at Ephesus, Paul said, "Wives, submit yourselves unto your own husbands, as unto the Lord" (Eph. 5:22). In this chapter in Ephesians Paul uses husband and wife to illustrate the true meaning of the New Testament Church: Christ is head of the Church and we are members of His body. The husband is head of the woman, and true marriage in God's sight makes man and woman one in the Lord—"they are no longer twain, but *one flesh*." A born again wife does not find it difficult to be in subjection to a born again husband. She is willing for the husband to be head of the household and make the final decisions in matters pertaining to the home and the life of each member of the family.

Verse 19: "Husbands, love your wives, and be not bitter against them."

Paul admonishes the wives to be in submission to the husbands, and do it as unto the Lord, for His sake and for His glory. Then he immediately commands the husband to love the wife and not be bitter against her. The husband is the head and commander-in-chief of the home, but he is not to be a bully—he is to rule in kindness and love.

Paul lived in the day of slavery, and in that day some men counted a wife as no more than a legal concubine; they did not marry because of love and devotion. Some men had several wives, and they were no more than servants and tools in the hands of bitter and ungodly men. However—if a man had been born again, if he were risen with Christ, he must have but one wife and he was to love, honor and cherish her. In the same manner, a wife must submit to her own husband—not to *another woman's husband*, but to her own; there is to be no practice of bigamy in the New Testament Church. Paul forbids a believing husband in the Church to be harsh and unkind in word or deed as having to do with his wife. He must deal with her in love and tender compassion.

There are not enough adjectives or words in all the languages of all the world to express the happiness of a true marriage in the Lord—a marriage according to God's divine formula for marriage and the home, a marriage which is of the Lord according to His Word, recognized by God the Father—entered into by two born again believers who are one in hope, one in love, one in faith, one in discipline, one in service, one in spirit and (according to the Genesis account of marriage) *one in flesh*. They pray together, worship together, eat together, play together, sing songs together. Neither conceals anything from the other, neither willingly avoids the other, neither is a burden to the other. When one is sick, the other is sick also because of deep compassion and love.

One sacrifices for the other—and to sum it all up, EACH lives for the OTHER! Such a union in marriage is of the Lord—and where HE is, there is joy unspeakable and full of glory. Such a home is a suburb of heaven.

God first dwelt in the *home* (the home of Adam and Eve); but Satan broke the union between God and man in the home. It takes *godly homes* to make *churches*; it takes godly churches to make a great nation. The devil does not begin his destruction of a nation in its capital among the leaders of that nation; he begins in the homes—on the hillsides, in the valleys, in the cities. If Satan can wreck the home life he can undermine any nation, whether it be Greece, Rome, or the great United States of America!

Verse 20: "Children, obey your parents in all things: for this is well pleasing unto the Lord.

I firmly believe that if dad and mother are Christians, if they show respect for *each other* and govern their children in a Christian spirit, the children will automatically respect and obey such parents. We have many disobedient children today because they learned disobedience in the home. If such is not true in your case, this is not meant for you: but I believe God's promise: "Train up a child in the way he should go: and when he is old, he will not depart from it" (Prov. 22:6).

If a child loves and respects his parents as he should, such love will naturally lead to obedience. Only an *unnatural* child becomes a rebel in the home. The truth set forth here by the Apostle Paul is that children are not to judge whether they should or should not obey their parents; God Almighty settled that: *"Children, obey your parents in all things"* is a definite command of God that children respect their parents, and the last part of the verse tells us why: *"For this is well pleasing unto the Lord."*

In Ephesians 6:1–3 Paul gives more specific instructions on this same subject: "Children, obey your parents *in the Lord*: for this is right. Honour thy father and mother; which is the first commandment *with promise*; that it may be well with thee, and thou mayest *live long on the earth*."

Some young man or young lady may read these lines, whose dad (and perhaps mother, too) is a drunkard, a doper, or an outrageous sinner; and that young person may be asking, "Suppose my dad commands me to drink beer? Or to attend nightclubs and dancehalls in sinful company? In such cases, am I to obey my father in the flesh?"

The command to children is that they obey their parents in all things, "for this is well pleasing unto the Lord." Would it be "well pleasing unto the Lord" for you to drink intoxicants when you know such indulgence is wrong? Would it be "well pleasing to God" for you to yield your body into the arms of an unbeliever whose heart was filled with lust? Certainly such *would not* be well pleasing to the Lord. The Scriptural answer to such a question is found in the Scripture just quoted from Ephesians 6:1: "Children, obey your parents IN THE LORD, FOR THIS IS RIGHT!" That settles it. A child is to obey the parents insofar as that obedience will please God; but when parents command or direct a child to serve sin and lust, sell his soul to the devil and burn in hell, that child is to remember that he owes his life to God, and that he is to give Him first place in everything. Young people, obey your parents *in the Lord*, but never obey them in the devil.

Verse 21: "Fathers, provoke not your children to anger, lest they be discouraged."

Children are a blessing from God, and *babies make*

201

a house a home. I know there are some dear couples who can never know the joy of having their own child; but a marriage is never what it could have been until there are children. Love can never reach its highest heights nor joy know its utmost fullness until the voice of a baby is heard in the home. However, it is a great and grave responsibility to bring children into this world, and such responsibility is not to be taken lightly; it is to be taken with all the seriousness God can give to prospective parents.

When a baby is born, the parents of that child will be greatly responsible for what he or she becomes as an adult. We are commanded to train up a child in the way he should go, and we are also *warned*, "He that spareth the rod hateth his son." We are commanded to chasten and correct our children. Hebrews 12:6 plainly tells us that *God chastens every child whom He receives*, and if *God* chastens us as His children, there has never been a normal child born on the face of this earth who did not need correction from earthly parents at one time or another.

However, a parent should never mete out punishment in anger nor as the result of anger; a child should be chastened in reason and with moderation—never unmercifully, and never in public. The child should not feel that the chastisement is only a result of a parent's fretful anger; and obedience should not be prompted or forced by fear. If a child's best efforts can only receive a parental frown, but are never greeted with a parental smile, then his spirit is broken and he becomes discouraged. Never provoke your children to anger, and never whip a child just enough to make him mad; give a substantial correction. *Pray about it,* and the Holy Spirit will lead you in the matter of discipline for your child.

To the believers at Ephesus Paul said, "Ye fathers,

provoke not your children to wrath: but bring them up in the nurture and admonition of the Lord" (Eph. 6:4). The spirit of a young child is to be carefully and tenderly developed. One cannot crush the spirit of a child with harshness and lack of understanding, and expect that child to develop into a gracious, Christian lady or gentleman. With caution, a tender twig can be bent and shaped; but hasty, rude bending will warp or break such tender growth.

The grand and glorious duty (and opportunity) of every parent is to train up their children in the way they should go—in the nurture and admonition of the Lord, pointing them to God in tender years, laying heavily upon their trusting hearts that they should enlist in the army of the Lord and become a good soldier of Jesus Christ— not only to make sure of heaven, but also to be successful in life here on earth. Duty to God and to His Word and to the Church should be deeply impressed upon the heart of a child. Parents should warn their children concerning the lust of the flesh, the wiles of the devil and the cesspools of iniquity, urging them to surrender all to Jesus, who gave all for them; and when parents fulfill this duty as they should, that child in later years will "rise up to call them blessed!"

Verse 22: "Servants, obey in all things your masters according to the flesh; not with eyeservice, as menpleasers; but in singleness of heart, fearing God."

All believers are admonished to let the Word of God dwell in them richly; and whatsoever the believer does, all should be done in the name of the Lord Jesus, giving thanks to God and the Father BY the Lord Jesus.

A believing wife should submit to her own husband; a husband should love, honor and cherish his wife with tenderness.

Children are to obey their parents *in the Lord* in

all things because this is "well pleasing unto the Lord."

Fathers should never provoke their children to anger, lest the child become discouraged and lose the desire to be what he would otherwise be, for God and for himself.

Paul then moves from the immediate family to the servants. The servant is not to just obey his master with "eyeservice"—that is, he is not to be a diligent worker only while the master is looking on, but the servant who is born again is to be just as diligent when his master is many miles away. Primarily, Christian servants are not serving their *master in the flesh*, even though they may be working in his plant or on his farm: they are actually *serving God* in the position they occupy— not pleasing men with eyeservice, but doing all things from the heart, fearing God, knowing that *God is the Timekeeper* and that He keeps a perfect record. There are no mistakes in God's books, and His all-seeing eye misses nothing.

In Paul's day there were Christian slaves, and they were to work according to Christian principles. They were to do their duty at all times; they were to work with higher motive than just that of pleasing their earthly masters; they were at all times to be "fearing God," standing in awe of His authority over them. They were not to fear their earthly masters, but rather they were to fear God; and believing slaves would not strive to be men-pleasers if they recognized and surrendered to Christ's authority over them. Thus they would perform all duties with singleness of heart, as unto the Lord and not unto man. Regardless of who you are or where you are employed, according to Dr. Bob Jones, Sr., founder of Bob Jones University and a great saint of God, "IT IS A SIN TO DO LESS THAN YOUR BEST!"

Verse 23: "And whatsoever ye do, do it heartily, as

to the Lord, and not unto men."

The believers in Colosse were to labor at any task that might be assigned to them by their masters; to diligently work out that task without grumbling or reluctance— not only doing it honestly, but cheerfully and "heartily, as unto the Lord." The heathen slave might do his work with reluctance and with a grudge against his master, with no interest whatsoever in his labor; but the Christian slave or servant, having been made a new creation in Christ Jesus, was to act with cheerfulness, toil with cheerfulness, with careful attention to his task, for HE was serving no human master—but the Lord who bought him . . . not with corruptible things such as silver and gold, but with His own precious blood. Realizing this, there would be no temptation to fall into eyeservice, pleasing men instead of *doing all to the glory of God.*

The *immediate* object of the service rendered by a believer to his earthly master must be to *man*; but the *ultimate* object of that service is *unto the Lord* and should always be from the heart.

Verse 24: "Knowing that of the Lord ye shall receive the reward of the inheritance: for ye serve the Lord Christ."

Paul knew that if the Colossian believers had this persuasion within themselves, they would be able to follow the inspired admonition given to them, knowing that they would receive a reward at the end of life's journey. If they knew that in serving man they were serving God and would receive their rewards from *Him*, then serving their earthly masters would be much easier and could be done with joy not possible without the assurance of greater pay than that received from their immediate masters.

Christ, not man, will bestow the final reward upon all believers; and if we do no more than give one cup of cold water in the name of Jesus, we will not lose the reward for that. Believers have an inheritance—"undefiled, that fadeth not away, reserved in heaven," where thieves do not break through and steal, where moths do not corrupt nor rust destroy. Read Ephesians 1:11–14; Colossians 1:12; II Corinthians 5:5; I Peter 1:4.

These Colossian servants had no inheritance on earth, nothing they could call their own. They owned no property and no riches awaited them. But as believers they had a *hope*: They were to work faithfully, joyfully, untiringly; they were to suffer and wait patiently; and at the end of life's journey they would come into their eternal inheritance and reward, *"knowing that whatsoever good thing any man doeth, the same shall he receive of the Lord, whether he be bond or free"* (Eph. 6:8).

Verse 24 contains assurance: "KNOWING that of the Lord ye shall receive the reward . . . ." Believers KNOW that the Lord will reward in righteousness. He has promised; and since the Lord cannot break His promise, since He gives a reward so rich, so blessed, so full . . . *Serve ye Him*! Servants are to look above and beyond earthly things and human service; and looking up instead of looking *around*, the bright prospect of the eternal reward at the end of a life of service in the Lord Jesus will give joy that is unspeakable and full of glory!

Paul is impressing upon the hearts of the Christian slaves in the community at Colosse the fact that earthly masters do not have absolute right over a slave; the money paid him by the master gives title only over the *body* with its strength and physical labor; but believers were bought by the Lord Jesus at the tremendous price of His blood, and He therefore has the right to claim your homage and service. After we have done all that is commanded us, we are to say, "We are unprofitable servants. We have done that which was our duty."

Believers are to present their bodies a living sacrifice, holy and acceptable unto God, "which is our reasonable service." God has a perfect right to demand our all, for He GAVE all that we might be saved. Therefore, whatsoever we do as a believer, we are to do it as unto Him, knowing that He will reward us for any and all faithful stewardship.

Verse 25: "But he that doeth wrong shall receive for the wrong which he hath done: and there is no respect of persons."

The clear, understandable language of this verse makes it plain that the wrongdoer shall bear the penalty for the wrong he does. Whatsoever a man sows, that shall he also reap. They who sow to the flesh will reap corruption. The warning of this verse, I believe, is directed to the masters of the servants. Paul has instructed believing servants to give their very best in service, and then if the master mistreats them he will be dealt with by Almighty God.

Paul is saying to the believers in the Colossian church, "You are actually servants of the Lord Jesus Christ, and you shall receive due reward from Him. In the meantime, you may receive injustice and wrong from your earthly masters; they may underpay you and abuse you; but rest assured they will be judged for that—not by an earthly judge, but by the Righteous Judge whose decision knows no respect of persons. So give of your best to your immediate masters."

To the slave masters he says, "You masters give to your servants what is just and right, for if you treat them wrongly God will judge you and give you your just due, because God looks upon your *servants* with just as much honor and respect as that with which He looks upon *you.* God knows no respect of persons."

The truth in this verse is a general truth. Today's application would be to men who are the overseers or employers of daily laborers in some of the corporations of our land. Any person who works at public work should give honest hours and honest labor to his employer; *any believer who does less than that* is sinning; he is stealing time from his employer. But if the employer fails to pay his employees as they should be paid, the *employer* is sinning and God will judge him for his unrighteous dealings. Read Ephesians 6:9; Romans 2:11; Acts 10:34; James 2:1–9.

COLOSSIANS -- CHAPTER FOUR

1. Masters, give unto your servants that which is just and equal; knowing that ye also have a Master in heaven.

2. Continue in prayer, and watch in the same with thanksgiving;

3. Withal praying also for us, that God would open unto us a door of utterance, to speak the mystery of Christ, for which I am also in bonds:

4. That I may make it manifest, as I ought to speak.

5. Walk in wisdom toward them that are without, redeeming the time.

6. Let your speech be alway with grace, seasoned with salt, that ye may know how ye ought to answer every man.

7. All my state shall Tychicus declare unto you, who is a beloved brother, and a faithful minister and fellowservant in the Lord:

8. Whom I have sent unto you for the same purpose, that he might know your estate, and comfort your hearts;

9. With Onesimus, a faithful and beloved brother, who is one of you. They shall make known unto you all things which are done here.

10. Aristarchus my fellowprisoner saluteth you, and Marcus, sister's son to Barnabas, (touching whom ye received commandments: if he come unto you, receive him;)

11. And Jesus, which is called Justus, who are of the circumcision. These only are my fellowworkers unto the kingdom of God, which have been a comfort unto me.

12. Epaphras, who is one of you, a servant of Christ, saluteth you, always labouring fervently for you in prayers, that ye may stand perfect and complete in all the will of God.

13. For I bear him record, that he hath a great zeal for you, and them that are in Laodicea, and them in Hierapolis.

14. Luke, the beloved physician, and Demas, greet you.

15. Salute the brethren which are in Laodicea, and Nymphas, and the church which is in his house.

16. And when this epistle is read among you, cause that it be read also in the church of the Laodiceans; and that ye likewise read the epistle from Laodicea.

17. And say to Archippus, Take heed to the ministry which thou hast received in the Lord, that thou fulfil it.

18. The salutation by the hand of me Paul. Remember my bonds. Grace be with you. Amen.

"Masters, give unto your servants that which is just and equal; knowing that ye also have a Master in heaven."

This is a continuation of the truth set forth in the last verse of chapter 3. Paul has instructed the servants how to behave toward their masters, and whether the masters are believers or unbelievers does not change the responsibility of the believing slave. Paul also admonished the master how to conduct himself toward his slaves, and his conduct is not to be determined by whether or not the slave is a believer or an unbeliever. The admonition is given to Christian slaves and Christian masters.

Some of the Christian slaves might have heathen masters, or a believing master might have unbelieving slaves. Regardless of whether the servant is serving a believing or an unbelieving master does not change his responsibility in faithful and joyous service; and the believing master who has unbelievers in his company of slaves is not to mistreat the unbeliever nor render unto him less than unto his believing slaves. The slave is to give his best to his master—not only to please *him*, but also TO PLEASE THE LORD. Likewise, the master is to give the slave all to which he is entitled—not just to please the servant, but to please God, doing it "heartily, as unto the Lord."

Paul warned the masters, *"Knowing that ye also have a Master in heaven."* He wanted the masters to realize the solemn fact that Christian slaves and Christian slavemasters were ransomed by the same blood, members of the same body through the baptism of the Holy Spirit, having the same service appointed to them and the same prospect set before them; that master and slave would stand on the same level in the same judgment day, to receive an eternal inheritance in which they would share equally, regardless of the difference of social rank here on earth. If the masters understood this solemn scriptural truth, then they would not be tempted to treat their slaves with harshness nor steal from them by withholding goods or wages.

Job cried out, "If I did despise the cause of my manservant or of my maidservant, when they contended with me; what then shall I do when GOD RISETH UP? And when He visiteth, what shall I answer Him? Did not He that made me in the womb make him? And did not one fashion us in the womb?" (Job 31:13–15).

In the day of the Apostle Paul, so numerous were the slaves that in some communities slaves outnumbered free men four to one. Probably in all of the early churches there were many born again slaves. In the Colossian letter, Paul lays down three solemn Bible facts that are fatal to slavery:

1.   He denied a common theory of his day which declared slaves—whether born into slavery or brought into slavery because of mental status—to be inferior to their masters. Paul discredited this and admits no distinction but the one of accidental rank.

2.   He declared that certain duties to slaves by their masters should be performed from natural right. This teaching finally caused born again slavemasters to free their slaves, who were themselves created in the image of God and entitled to personal freedom.

3.   Paul clearly taught that in the New Testament Church there is no such thing as bond or free, that Christian masters and their believing slaves were members of the same body—the New Testament Church of which Jesus is the head; and that slaves set free by the Son of God were free indeed!

Christianity and slavery cannot coexist. When slave-

211

masters become born again Christians they automatically free their slaves. All men on this earth are created free and equal, and no man has any right to own the body of his fellowman. Every man has a right to his personal liberty so long as he is not a menace to society. Paul preached Christian liberty and Christian freedom, and he clearly instructed slaves and masters in their Christian duty toward each other.

Verse 2: "Continue in prayer, and watch in the same with thanksgiving."

Beginning with verse 2, Paul gives more general admonitions; but notice that he places prayer first. Paul was a man of prayer. In Ephesians 6:18 we read, "Praying always with all prayer and supplication in the Spirit, and watching thereunto with all perseverance and supplication for all saints."

To the Romans Paul said, "Rejoicing in hope; patient in tribulation; continuing instant in prayer" (Rom. 12:12). Writing to the believers at Thessalonica he commanded, "PRAY WITHOUT CEASING" (I Thess. 5:17). Paul did not want his children in the Lord to entertain the idea that prayer was ever needless. Even if they did not stand in need of any particular spiritual or temporal blessing, they were to be faithful in prayer, thanking God at all times for His manifold blessings.

Perseverance in prayer proves the sincerity of faith on the part of the believer, and those who diligently seek God will always receive an answer. According to Paul's teaching, believers are to pray and wait; never to become discouraged, but hold on in prayer in the spirit of the man who said, "I WILL NOT LET THEE GO EXCEPT THOU BLESS ME!" (Gen. 32:26).

"*Watch in the same with thanksgiving.*" That is, watch in prayer, with thanksgiving. Paul did not want the Colossian believers to become careless or spiritually lazy. He wanted them to beware of spiritual drowsiness in their devotions and in their prayer life. As they prayed they were to be alert and wide awake, "in thanksgiving." Prayers that reach the throne of God are prayed by Christians who give themselves with sleepless anxiety, watching and fervently interceding until the answer comes. It may not be the answer desired or expected—but if God says, "No," to the Spirit-filled believer, that is the answer that should be willingly accepted with thanksgiving. Sometimes all God gives in answer to our prayer is a simple "No," because He knows what is best for us.

Paul impressed upon the hearts of the Colossians that they were to be thankful. We must give due credit to Him, for He is the giver of every good and perfect gift. In prayer we must thank Him for what He has already done before we ask Him to do more. There are so many reasons for thanksgiving, and certainly not the least of them is the privilege of prayer. True prayer and thanksgiving coexist in the heart of a born again believer. "In everything give thanks: for this is the will of God in Christ Jesus concerning you" (I Thess. 5:18).

Verse 3: "Withal praying also for us, that God would open unto us a door of utterance, to speak the mystery of Christ, for which I am also in bonds."

Paul wished himself to be a special object of the prayers of the Colossian Christians. He wanted them to pray that God would open unto him "a door of utterance"; but he was not selfish in his request—he included others. He said, "Praying also for US, that God would open unto US a door." Timothy is no doubt one of those included in this request, and possibly others who are named in this fourth chapter.

Paul knew the power of prayer! The prayer of Elijah,

213

a man like unto ourselves, shut up heaven for the space of three years, and it rained not. The same man prayed again and it rained. At the voice of a man in prayer, the sun stood still. Prayer sweetened the bitter fountains of water and divided the Red Sea. Prayer has disbanded armies, prevented wars, shortened battles and brought victory to the righteous. Prayer has brought temporal blessings in abundance, as in the case of Jabez (I Chron. 4:10). Prayer brought healing and added fifteen years to the life of Hezekiah. Prayer stopped the mouths of lions, quenched the violence of fire, opened the gates of a prison for Peter. Jesus prayed on the Mount of Transfiguration, and His raiment became white and glistening while His face shone like the sun! The glory of God was manifested to Moses when he prayed. The grace of Christ was made manifest to Paul when he besought it. The thief on the cross prayed, and Jesus took him that same day to Paradise. A messenger from heaven stood right beside Daniel when he finished praying his daily devotions. The invitation to the believer concerning prayer is simple and easily understood:

"What things soever ye desire, when ye pray, believe that ye receive them, and ye shall have them!" (Mark 11:24). "If two of you shall agree on earth as touching any thing that they shall ask, it shall be done for them of my Father which is in heaven" (Matt. 18:19). Jesus said, "Ask, and it shall be given you; seek, and ye shall find; knock, and it shall be opened unto you" (Matt. 7:7).

Paul wanted the church in Colosse to pray that God would open the door and give him an opportunity to preach the unsearchable riches of God's grace. It is true he had limited opportunity to witness in his confinement, but he longed to be out of prison, to have the liberty of traveling through the countryside preaching the precious Gospel of salvation.

214

Paul was not grumbling because his personal liberty had been taken away; he was not praying to be released from jail simply for the sake of being out of bondage. He wanted the Colossians to pray that God would open the door of opportunity to preach in the streets, in the market places, and throughout the cities as he had done heretofore. He assured them that he would preach the same Gospel he had opened up unto them, "to speak the mystery of Christ," and they knew exactly what he meant by that. The Lord Jesus Christ is the subject of that mystery. It has its theme in Christ and it was the Apostle's message to kings, commoners, slaves and slavemasters alike. To Paul, the Gospel was the incarnation, the crucifixion, the burial, resurrection and personal return of Jesus to receive His own.

The last part of verse 3 reveals the reason for Paul's being in prison: ". . . for which I am also in bonds." He was in jail for preaching the mystery—"Christ in you, the hope of glory"—kings and paupers, slavemasters and slaves, Jews and Greeks all in one body. Paul was in prison for preaching this very message; yet he made it plain that if set free HE WOULD PREACH IT AGAIN! Thus, he sends a request to the believers to pray for him that he WILL be set free so that he can preach again the same message that caused him to be put in bonds! His shackles had not deadened his love for the Gospel, nor his determination to preach it again, openly and boldly.

Paul was the minister to the Gentiles. He preached the Gospel to them, and his admission of these converted heathen into the church without following the rituals of the Mosaic Law had brought wrath down upon him. He was in jail because he had taken a firm stand that Gentiles, Jews, and "whosoever" are saved by grace through faith plus nothing. Therefore the Gentile Colossians had a special reason to remember him in their prayers. All

215

Gentiles are indebted to the Apostle Paul more than to any other person who ever lived, apart from the Lord Jesus Christ. As the called and commissioned Apostle to the Gentiles, he gloried in his ministry.

Paul suffered as none other, to make known the Gospel of the grace of God to the Gentiles. He was persecuted—but he continued to labor to turn the Gentiles from darkness to light, and to make known to us the knowledge of salvation through the grace of God. He preached repentance toward God, faith in the finished work of the Lord Jesus—and made plain the fact that one repenting in godly sorrow, believing with all his heart that Christ died for his sins, was buried and rose again according to the Scriptures, becomes a member of the body of which Jesus Christ is the head. We Gentiles learned the glorious truth through Paul's ministry. He was very dear to the hearts of the Colossians, and our own memory of him should be sweet.

Verse 4: "That I may make it manifest, as I ought to speak."

Paul wanted the Colossians to pray that God would open the door of liberty in order that he might be free to preach the Gospel, but he wanted them to pray further that God would give him the boldness he had always had in preaching. This does not mean that Paul was entertaining the idea of compromising the Gospel, but he knew he was in a body of flesh and had suffered great agony of body for the sake of the Gospel. He therefore urged the Colossians to pray that he might preach as he ought to preach—with boldness. We know that this bore heavily upon the heart of Paul, because two times he asked the church at Ephesus to pray for him, that he might speak with boldness. He described himself as "an ambassador in bonds" (Eph. 6:20).

Paul was a spiritual giant, but pain and continual

216

suffering can wear down even such a one. He had suffered pain and agony for the Gospel, such as you and I will never know; and he urged his children in the Lord to intercede in his behalf, that God would open the door for him that he might preach the grace of God again, and that when the door was opened he would have holy boldness to preach with the same fervor and sincerity as in the early days of his ministry.

As I write these lines, I have been preaching the Gospel for more than 28 years, and I have never compromised the pure Gospel for any reason; but I am a man, I am in the flesh. I need the prayers of my friends who hear the radio broadcasts, who read my sermons in print, and who attend my meetings. Will you please *pray for me*, that God will keep me true and faithful to His pure, unadulterated Word? I could have larger crowds at my meetings and a great deal more money, if I would preach to please people; but will you pray that God will keep me strong in heart and body, and that He will give me holy boldness to preach the grace of God, the blood of Jesus, the virgin birth, the premillennial return of Christ— the cardinal truths of the Church? Pray that God will keep me faithful and, in the words of the Apostle Paul, "that I may make the Gospel manifest as I ought to speak."

Verse 5: "Walk in wisdom toward them that are without, redeeming the time."

The statement "them that are without" is found in I Corinthians 5:12 and also in I Thessalonians 4:12. It refers to persons outside the Church—unbelievers; and not just to false teachers as some Bible scholars suggest. The unbelievers without (outside the Church) should be surrounded on the part of believers with every inducement to become a believer and come into the true Church. Nothing should be said or done by a believer that would stand in the way of sinners. Believers should live a life that would exhibit to unbelievers that Christianity is genuine and is everything the Word of God claims it to be.

There are many things a believer can do, many places a believer can go, and not lose his redemption or burn in the pits of hell at the end of life's journey; but believers should "walk in wisdom." They should be very careful what they do, what they say and where they go. Paul said, "If meat make my brother to offend, I will eat no flesh while the world standeth, lest I make my brother to offend" (I Cor. 8:13). Believers are the world's Bible. Those of us who profess to be followers of the Lord Jesus are watched and observed in all that we do. We should be very, very careful how we conduct ourselves at all times, every moment of every day, but especially when we are in the presence of unbelievers.

The "wisdom" here referred to is more than abstaining from questionable acts. It also means that Christians should use wisdom in trying to win sinners to Jesus. Jesus cautioned, "Be wise as serpents, and harmless as doves" (Matt. 10:16). Many times zeal without knowledge does more eternal damage than eternal good. Someone has stated it thus: "Zeal without knowledge is as the thundershower that drenches and injures—not as the rain which with noiseless and gentle descent softens, fertilizes and causes to grow."

The Lord Jesus Christ said, "Give not that which is holy unto the dogs, neither cast ye your pearls before swine, lest they trample them under their feet, and turn again and rend you" (Matt. 7:6).

In I Thessalonians 5:19 Paul admonishes, "Quench not the Spirit." We should never quench the Spirit; we should be led of the Spirit at all times, and if we are led by the Holy Spirit to speak to someone who is an un-

218

believer, the Spirit will prepare the way and cause the unbeliever to be willing to listen. But if we try to force our Christian convictions upon those who are unconcerned and haughty, we are casting the pearls of the Gospel before swine, and such is not pleasing to the Lord. There are many Christians who need to seek God's will concerning the method used in attempting to win souls.

Verse 5 closes with the words, "Redeeming the time." Paul simply means by this statement that believers are to buy up every opportunity to witness to unbelievers, thereby redeeming the time.

Most of us do not fully realize what grand and glorious opportunity God has afforded us in permitting us to win souls, and we will never know this side of eternity the value of one soul. Jesus illustrates thus: "What shall a man be profited, if he shall gain the whole world, and lose his own soul?" (Matt. 16:26).

Can you envision all the wealth of all the world in one great mountainous heap, with *one soul* weighed against such a peak of silver and gold? Yet Jesus declared that one soul is worth MORE than all the wealth of all the world. Those of us who pass unbelievers by, failing to witness to them and point them to the Lord Jesus Christ as Saviour, are passing up pearls and diamonds—jewels that are invaluable. Wasting time is a sin of great magnitude.

"To him that knoweth to do good and doeth it not, to him it is sin" (James 4:17). Solomon, the man of wisdom, said, "He that winneth souls is wise." Daniel said, "They that be wise shall shine as the brightness of the firmament; and they that turn many to righteousness as the stars for ever and ever." The biggest and most profitable business on this earth is that of winning souls, and every believer should be a soul winner. God does not call all believers to preach or pastor a church, nor to leave their home and go to the mission fields; but *God saves to serve,* and He has never saved any person to just sit down and rest while sinners pour into hell by the millions! We are to buy up every opportunity to tell men about Jesus and point them to the Christ who died to save to the uttermost all who will come unto God by Him.

Verse 6: "Let your speech be alway with grace, seasoned with salt, that ye may know how ye ought to answer every man."

Believers should be very careful how they speak. In the original Greek, the idea set forth here is that believers should not speak with terseness nor with the attitude of a "smart aleck." We should be humble, kind and agreeable, so long as our humility, kindness and affability do not lead to compromise and indifference. Under no condition is a believer to compromise fundamental truth and godly convictions, but neither are we to be stubborn, terse, nor smart in our talk—especially with unbelievers. We are to speak "that which is good to the use of edifying."

To drive the truth deeper into the hearts of the Colossians Paul used a term they fully understood: "seasoned with salt." In the Sermon on the Mount, Jesus told His disciples, "Ye are the salt of the earth." Salt purifies, preserves and sweetens. In the Scriptures, salt has various applications, such as the salt of the covenant and the salt of the sacrifice. Salt symbolizes preserving, purifying, preventing decay or deterioration. It is a symbol of spiritual purification, and Christianity is the force on earth today that keeps civilization from decaying. Take all Christianity out of a nation and what do you have? The people become savages who practice all the laws of the jungle. Christians are to speak words "seasoned with salt."

In Ephesians 4:29 Paul says, "Let no corrupt communication proceed out of your mouth, but that which is good to the use of edifying, that it may minister grace to the hearers."

". . . That ye may know how ye ought to answer every man." Believers must be very careful how they speak to one another, and especially how they answer unbelievers concerning things having to do with this life and with spiritual life. In admonishing believers concerning their speech, Paul is thinking primarily of those without the Church, because he knows that *unbelievers* will judge the Lord Jesus by the action and language of *believers*. Solomon said, "DEATH AND LIFE ARE IN THE POWER OF THE TONGUE" (Prov. 18:21). The same answer will not suffice for all, and we must answer individuals in wisdom. Therefore, our speech must be seasoned with salt and our words baptized in grace if we would be "wise as serpents and harmless as doves."

In Luke 9:9 we read, "And Herod said, John have I beheaded: but who is this, of whom I hear such things? And he desired to see (Jesus)." In Luke 23:8–9 the story continues: "And when Herod saw Jesus, he was exceeding glad: for he was desirous to see Him of a long season, because he had heard many things of Him; and he hoped to have seen some miracle done by Him. Then he questioned with Him in many words; *but He (Jesus) answered him (Herod) nothing!*"

Remember . . . *remember*!! "*Cast not your pearls before swine!*" Herod beheaded John the Baptist. He was a very wicked, ungodly man, and no doubt he had crossed God's deadline. He questioned Jesus "in many words," but Jesus answered him *not one word*. Yet we

221

read, in verses 39—43 of the same chapter, "And one of the malefactors which were hanged railed on Him, saying, If thou be Christ, save thyself and us. But the other answering rebuked Him, saying, Dost not thou fear God, seeing thou art in the same condemnation? And we indeed justly; for we receive the due reward of our deeds: but this man hath done nothing amiss. And he said unto Jesus, LORD, REMEMBER ME WHEN THOU COMEST INTO THY KINGDOM. And Jesus said unto him, VERILY I SAY UNTO THEE, TO DAY SHALT THOU BE WITH ME IN PARADISE."

In the same chapter of God's holy Word, Jesus refuses to utter one single word to a godless king who had beheaded Christ's forerunner and had persecuted the saints. The only reason he wanted to see the Lord was because he thought he might see Him work a miracle. Therefore Jesus did not say one word to Herod. But a dying thief (who confessed his sin and confessed that he was worthy of death) spoke nine words to Jesus. Jesus heard and answered him—and carried him that day into the Paradise of God.

Read I Peter 1:15 and 3:1; II Tim. 2:25—26. According to these passages, meekness is one special element of the Christian answer to those without (outside) the Church.

CHRISTIAN FELLOWSHIP

Paul did not wish to burden the Colossian Epistle with lengthy details of his private affairs. The believers in that church were deeply interested in his health, his sufferings and his plans; but the bearer of the Epistle would make known to them orally the answers to any questions they might ask, and would inform them concerning the health and general condition of the aging saint as he sat in prison in Rome.

Verse 7: "All my state shall Tychicus declare unto you, who is a beloved brother, and a faithful minister and fellowservant in the Lord."

Paul must have loved Tychicus very dearly—he honors him with mention in three of his epistles. First he is called "a beloved brother," one of the sacred brotherhood in the Lord, bound together in Christ with bonds of divine love. Paul was an outstanding apostle, but he never felt superior to the brethren. He owned and loved as a brother everyone who was a true believer, but it seems that Tychicus had endeared himself to Paul and that he was rewarded with highest respect and confidence. As a trusted servant of God he carried the Epistle to the Colossians and was trusted with an oral message to the believers there.

In Ephesians, Tychicus is called "a beloved brother and faithful minister in the Lord," and here in Colossians Paul refers to him as "a fellowservant in the Lord." To Paul this man was beloved, trustworthy, a faithful fellowservant and a co-laborer.

Verse 8: "Whom I have sent unto you for the same purpose, that he might know your estate, and comfort your hearts."

What Paul is saying is simply this: "I know you are concerned about me, I know your hearts are burdened because I am in prison—but I am not writing concerning my private sufferings and personal affairs. Tychicus, whom I trust and love, will tell you all about me. You may depend upon what he tells you, because he knows all about my sufferings and my situation here in prison."

"Know your estate"—that is, just how you are standing up under persecution, and if any have deviated in the least from the faith.

Verse 9: "With Onesimus, a faithful and beloved

brother, who is one of you. They shall make known unto you all things which are done here."

These two brethren, Tychicus and Onesimus, were traveling to Colosse. They were to deliver the Epistle to the Colossians and make known the condition of the aged and beloved Paul. However, Onesimus carried with him another and much more special message—a testimony and introduction to his former master, Philemon.

Onesimus had been a slave. He had run away and left his owner, but during his exile he had been converted under the ministry of Paul, who was now sending him back to Philemon a new man—no longer an unbelieving, unprofitable slave, but a new creation in Christ Jesus: "Not now as a servant, but above a servant, a brother beloved, specially to me, but how much more unto thee, both in the flesh, and in the Lord?" (Philemon 16).

It is true that Onesimus had been unfaithful to his master as a slave—he had run away, and that was a serious offence in that day of slavery; but regardless of what he had done in the past, he was now a new creation. Paul commends him as a faithful brother in the Lord and one with them in the body of Christ. "These two brethren," said Paul to the Colossians, "shall make known unto you all things which are done here."

Paul knew the anxiety the believers in the Colossian church had for him, and he wished to comfort them. He knew that Tychicus would tell them how he felt in his heart, and that he was looking forward to the day when the door of liberty would swing open, thus permitting him to again preach the Gospel of the grace of God. He also knew that when the believers learned that he was unshaken, unmoved, and still the same servant of God—beloved, faithful and true—they would be encouraged in the inner man.

Verse 10: "Aristarchus my fellowprisoner saluteth

you, and Marcus, sister's son to Barnabas (touching whom ye received commandments: if he come unto you, receive him)."

Aristarchus was of Macedonia, a native of Thessalonica. Read Acts 19:29; 20:4; 27:2; and Philemon 24. This fellowprisoner had been with Paul on many occasions before they were thrown into prison. They were together during the riot at Ephesus, and he had traveled with Paul several times on journeys to Syria and Greece. They were together when Paul sailed from Italy on his journey to make his appeal to Caesar, and it seems that this brother remained with Paul in Rome and now is in prison with him. Paul speaks of him here as a "fellowprisoner," but in Philemon as a "fellow-labourer." From such change in manner of address, it has been inferred that apparently there were no charges against him and that he had been released from prison. He was undoubtedly there with Paul because of his deep love for the aged apostle, remaining with him in jail to comfort and encourage him. What a brother! Thank God for Christians so unselfish, so much like the Christ they serve and follow!

My heart is humbled and I am extremely grateful to God for *my* friends who stand by me in prayer and in every way in which it is possible for one believer to stand by another. I am so glad to know that Paul had faithful friends who were even willing to sit in jail with him, to give him comfort and encouragement. Christians also have *God's* promise, "I will never leave thee, nor forsake thee. So that we may boldly say, The Lord is my helper, and I will not fear what man shall do unto me" (Heb. 13:5,6).

"Marcus" is no doubt John Mark, referred to in Acts 12:12–25; 13:5,13; 15:37,39; and II Tim. 4:11. This was the young man who caused a dispute and separation between Paul and Barnabas. On a former missionary journey Mark had left them and "went not with them to the work." Paul therefore thought it was unwise to take him with them again, "and the contention was so sharp between them, that they parted asunder one from the other" (Acts 15:39).

No one can say whether *Paul* or *Barnabas* was right in their respective opinions about Mark, but the fact that he deserted them on a missionary journey seems to justify Paul's opinion concerning him. But even though there may be division among truly born again believers, if fully surrendered to God's will they will come back together in Christian love and forgiveness, and Mark was reconciled to Paul some time later. It could be that the dispute between Paul and John Mark was used of the Holy Spirit to awaken Mark to his responsibilities and make of him a vessel well used of God, because Paul mentions Mark with great respect and words of high commendation in II Timothy 4:11: "Only Luke is with me. Take Mark, and bring him with thee: *for he is profitable to me for the ministry.*"

Barnabas was a wide-awake evangelist who was well known to the Colossians; they loved and respected him. By birth, Barnabas was a Levite. He was born on the Island of Cyprus and was converted to Christianity at a very early age. In adult years he sold his earthly possessions to become an evangelist, and it was he who introduced Paul to the church in Jerusalem. Barnabas was a man in whom the church had confidence. He was sent from the mother church to Antioch as a messenger to bring back the report of the Gospel in that city, and when he returned, here is the record:

"Who, when he (Barnabas) came, and had seen the grace of God, was glad, and exhorted them all, that with purpose of heart they would cleave unto the Lord. For he was a good man, and full of the Holy Ghost and of faith: and much people was added unto the Lord'' (Acts 11:23,24). The next verse tells us that Barnabas then went to Tarsus, returned with Paul, and their evangelistic labors were so successful that ''the disciples were called Christians first in Antioch.''

Barnabas then went up to Jerusalem carrying funds for the poor saints there, and he and Paul visited many communities together, preaching the Gospel. The church later selected Barnabas to go up to Jerusalem to settle an angry controversy concerning believers and the Law of Moses, after which he returned to Antioch; and we read that he was continually ''teaching and preaching the Word of the Lord.''

It was after this successful period of evangelistic meetings that Paul and Barnabas had their sharp contention about John Mark as a missionary companion. The last account we read of Barnabas in this episode tells us, ''And so Barnabas took Mark and sailed unto Cyprus.'' Paul mentions Mark in connection with Barnabas here in Colossians 4:10 to assure the believers at Colosse that they should receive Mark with open arms and a cordial Christian welcome, treating him as a true apostle and brother in the Lord.

Verse 10 closes with the words, ''. . . if he come unto you, receive him.'' Believers are prone to make mistakes. We live in a body of flesh and we may grievously fail the Lord and our fellow Christians; but if a believer fails—and repents of that failure, thereby proving himself—that believer should be forgiven and accepted again in full fellowship because we are members of the same body, and when one member of the body suffers, ALL the members suffer.

Paul had no doubt learned that Mark planned a

journey which would lead him through the city of Colosse, and if he did travel through that city the believers there were to receive and welcome him as a brother in the Lord, regardless of the misunderstanding and friction between Paul and Mark in their earlier missionary travels.

Verse 11: "And Jesus, which is called Justus, who are of the circumcision. These only are my fellowworkers unto the kingdom of God, which have been a comfort unto me."

We know nothing about this "Jesus which is called Justus." The statement "who are of the circumcision" refers to the three brethren named—Aristarchus, Mark and Jesus Justus. So far as we know, these three Jews were the only members of Paul's race who assisted him in Rome in his ministry in that wicked city; all other Jews would have nothing to do with him. But of these three men Paul says, "who have been a comfort unto me." (The literal Greek here reads, "Who indeed have been an encouragement to me.") The other believing Jews seemed to do all they could against Paul, and in Philippians he said of the Jewish believers that they preached Christ "even of envy and strife . . . of contention, not sincerely, supposing TO ADD AFFLICTION TO MY BONDS" (Phil. 1:15,16).

Paul was the Apostle to the Gentiles and was very zealous toward them. Because he had made this fact known, many of the Jews hated him and were very bitter toward him. Paul, however, had a deep burden for his people. In Romans 9:1–3 he confesses in essence that he would be willing to burn in hell if such sacrifice would save his people; but he knew that even if he *could* give his body to be burned, or if he could descend into the pit on their behalf, that would be of no avail, because Paul was a grace preacher and he knew that there remained "no more sacrifice." The blood had been shed once, for all, forever—and Jews and Gentiles alike must be saved by grace through faith plus nothing.

Verse 12: "Epaphras, who is one of you, a servant of Christ, saluteth you, always labouring fervently for you in prayers, that ye may stand perfect and complete in all the will of God."

The believers named in the remaining verses of the chapter were persons of heathen birth—not born of the Jews. Epaphras is referred to as "one of you." He was a Colossian; he was born there and was no doubt converted there. He naturally was deeply interested in his home church, and in this epistle he sends Christian greetings and love. Paul declares him to be a true minister of the Gospel, and it is entirely possible that God had used Epaphras in opening the door of the Colossian church. At any rate, he was a servant of Christ, one of their pastors, and had a deep spiritual concern for his brethren.

Paul describes this fellow minister as "ALWAYS LABOURING FERVENTLY FOR YOU IN PRAYERS." Epaphras was absent from the home church; he was in jail; but he had not forgotten his brothers and sisters in Christ. He labored for them in prayer. He possessed a deep, pure, spiritual love that brought about an agony of earnestness in prayer on their behalf. The burden of his heart concerning the Colossians was, "that ye may stand perfect and complete in all the will of God." Epaphras knew the danger to which the believers were exposed. He knew the subtleness of the error taught by the false teachers in Colosse, and he prayed for his brothers, that they would stand immovable, that they would not deviate from the faith. He wanted them to stand perfect, fully assured in the faith once delivered unto the saints. He wanted them to be continually yielded to "ALL THE WILL OF GOD."

Verse 13: "For I bear him record, that he hath a great zeal for you, and them that are in Laodicea, and them in Hierapolis."

Paul assured the believers in the Colossian church that Epaphras was zealous. The prison had not dampened his spirit nor quenched the fires that burned in his soul concerning the Gospel of grace in his home church, and the pangs and burdens of prayer that gripped his heart and soul were also extended to the Christians in Laodicea and Hierapolis—cities in the same region as Colosse. All three towns were in Phrygia. Epaphras well knew each church in that locality and no doubt had fellowshipped with them many times.

Verse 14: "Luke, the beloved physician, and Demas, greet you."

Paul's doctor (Luke) was with him. The health of the aged apostle had been carefully guarded by his physician, whom he terms *"the beloved physician."* Doctor Luke loved Paul and traveled with him on many, many occasions. He was with him as he traveled to Rome, and he remained there with him. Luke is also mentioned by Paul in his letter to Philemon (verse 24) and in II Timothy 4:11.

Who Demas was, we do not know; there is no explanation given. He is possibly the person later referred to in II Timothy 4:10: "For Demas hath forsaken me, having loved this present world." There could have been quite another verse here had Demas been faithful—first to the Lord and then to God's beloved Apostle Paul; but the glamor and lure of the world beckoned him away from Paul's side, and we have no record of what happened to him after that.

Verse 15: "Salute the brethren which are in Laodicea, and Nymphas, and the church which is in his house."

The believers in the Colossian church were to salute and thereby encourage the sister assembly, perhaps a weaker church in Laodicea—and especially were they to remember Nymphas, in whose home the church met. Some portion of the Laodicean believers, for what reason we know not, met regularly for worship in the house of Nymphas; and Paul, in mentioning his name, points out that Nymphas was worthy of distinction and a special greeting.

Verse 16: "And when this epistle is read among you, cause that it be read also in the church of the Laodiceans; and that ye likewise read the epistle from Laodicea."

In this verse Paul instructs the Colossian church to read the epistle in public, and recommends that they and the Laodiceans exchange letters, thus allowing each to be read in the assemblies of both churches.

Bible scholars agree that it is not known just what Paul means by the statement "that ye likewise read the epistle from Laodicea." There is no need to speculate concerning the matter. *Whatever* epistle the Laodiceans had in their assembly at the time was in turn to be sent to the Colossians and read in the church there.

Such interchange of letters was the custom among the churches, and by this system an epistle sent to one church became, in reality, the common property of ALL the churches. This led to the formation of the New Testament. Paul declares that "all Scripture is given by inspiration of God, and is profitable for doctrine, for reproof, for correction, for instruction in righteousness: that the man of God may be perfect, throughly furnished unto all good works" (II Tim. 3:16,17).

Verse 17: "And say to Archippus, Take heed to the ministry which thou hast received in the Lord, that thou fulfil it."

Archippus is also mentioned in Paul's letter to Philemon. What motive Paul had in sending a message directly to this believer we do not know. Whatever the ministry of Archippus was, it was a divine office which he had received "in the Lord," and he was to see to it that he fulfilled it (Acts 12:25). Whatever that ministry was, it was his duty to discharge the office he held in the Colossian church. It is generally supposed that Archippus had taken over the office of Epaphras, whose position in the church was left vacant because he was with Paul. Some Bible authorities say that Archippus was the son of Philemon, and that he was a deacon in the Colossian church.

It may well be that Paul sent the admonition openly, to be read to the church, in order that, should it become necessary for Archippus to correct or discipline some of the members, they would not become bitter against him and accuse him of assuming authority that was not his. They would remember Paul's charge to him and would respect and esteem him as God's servant because of Paul's appointing and admonishing him to "take heed to the ministry which thou hast received in the Lord, that thou fulfil it." They would listen to Archippus because of Paul's definite command to him to discharge his duties in the office to which he had been appointed.

Verse 18: "The salutation by the hand of me Paul. Remember my bonds. Grace be with you. Amen."

Paul had grown old. He was in jail now, and as the Holy Spirit dictated the words of this Epistle to him, someone else copied them on parchment; but after the main body of the letter was finished, Paul signed it with his own hand. Read I Corinthians 16:21; II Thessalonians 3:17.

Paul's "thorn in the flesh" (II Cor. 12:7) was believed by many scholars to have been cataracts or some disease of the eyes that had almost blinded him. How touching it must have been to the Colossians to see the handwriting of their beloved Paul! It may be that his signature was written in large letters, and as his dear sons and daughters in Christ read his name, their hearts ached as they remembered the wonderful days of fellowship when Paul came to Colosse and preached the wonderful Gospel that had rescued them from the slavery of sin.

Not only did he sign the letter in his own hand, but he added the closing request, *"Remember my bonds!"* A very brief request—but pathetic. It came from an anxious heart, from one who prayed daily that the door of liberty might again be opened for him and that he might again preach the glorious Gospel—the power of God unto salvation.

With every remembrance of his name he wanted them to remember his bonds. With every fond memory of days spent together when the church was born in Colosse, he wanted them to remember him now—in Rome, in bonds. When the assembly at Colosse met, rejoicing in religious liberty and freedom, Paul wanted them to remember that he was in prison, and the reason he was there was his message to the Gentiles: "In Christ all are one—Jew or Greek; slave or slavemaster; learned or unlearned—*whosoever.*" When the Colossian Christians prayed in the assembly or in the home, when they prayed for each other and for believers in other churches, Paul wanted them to be sure to "remember my bonds."

As Paul signed his name to the Colossian letter, small wonder that he was keenly aware of his bonds: as he wrote with his right hand, *his left hand was chained to a Roman guard!*

Conclusion to the letter is brief: "GRACE BE WITH YOU." This Epistle begins in grace and closes in grace:

233

in the very outset we read, "Paul, an apostle of Jesus Christ by the will of God, and Timotheus our brother, to the saints and faithful brethren in Christ which are at Colosse: *Grace be unto you.*"

Paul concludes this inspired message as he began it. Grace alone guarantees present and eternal spiritual blessings. We are SAVED by the grace of God (Eph. 2:8), we are TAUGHT by the grace of God (Titus 2:11–15), we OVERCOME by the grace of God—and no one knew that better than did Paul. After he prayed three times for God to remove the thorn from his flesh, God refused to remove the thorn but said to Paul, "MY GRACE IS SUFFICIENT FOR THEE, FOR MY STRENGTH IS MADE PERFECT IN WEAKNESS" (II Cor. 12:9).

Paul was a grace preacher. He was extremely jealous for the Lord Jesus Christ, who is "full of grace and truth" (John 1:14). He longed to see the believers at Galatia, Ephesus, Colosse and wherever God had used him to establish a church. He was jealous for his children in the Lord, and he prayed and admonished them often concerning false teachers—those who would mix law and grace, those who would deviate from pure grace, those who would rob the Lord Jesus of His finished work. Therefore he closes the Epistle to the Colossians, writing with his own hand: "Remember my bonds. Grace be with you. Amen!"

Dear reader, whoever you are, *do you know the grace of God*? Have you been saved by grace through faith? If you have not, you are lost. Regardless of your nationality, the color of your skin; regardless of your religious beliefs, your church affiliation or your sincerity—salvation is "not by works of righteousness which we have done" (Titus 3:5), but "by grace, through faith—and that not of ourselves." If you do not know beyond a shadow of a doubt that you are born again, bow your head and in your own words tell the Lord God that you are lost and that you want Jesus Christ to save you. Invite Him into your heart and life, believe on Him, trust Him, "and thou shalt be saved."

Then write me a note and tell me that you have been born again . . . I would love to share your joy with you. Your testimony is definitely my pay for the many hours I have spent in preparing this book.

May God bless you richly, my believing brother or sister. May He save you, is my prayer for each unbeliever into whose hands this book may fall.